W9-ASR-608

UNDERSTANDING

TENNESSEE WILLIAMS

Understanding Contemporary American Literature
Matthew J. Bruccoli, General Editor

Volumes on

Edward Albee • John Barth • Donald Barthelme
The Beats • The Black Mountain Poets
Robert Bly • Raymond Carver
Chicano Literature • Contemporary American Drama
Contemporary American Science Fiction
James Dickey • E. L. Doctorow • John Gardner
George Garrett • John Hawkes • Joseph Heller
John Irving • Randall Jarrell • William Kennedy
Ursula K. Le Guin • Denise Levertov • Bernard Malamud
Carson McCullers • Vladimir Nabokov • Joyce Carol Oates
Cynthia Ozick • Walker Percy • Katherine Anne Porter
Thomas Pynchon • Theodore Roethke • Philip Roth
Mary Lee Settle • Isaac Bashevis Singer • Gary Snyder
William Stafford • Anne Tyler • Kurt Vonnegut
Tennessee Williams

UNDERSTANDING
Tennessee
WILLIAMS

by ALICE GRIFFIN

UNIVERSITY OF SOUTH CAROLINA PRESS

Cloth edition published by the University of South Carolina Press, 1995
Paperback edition published in Columbia, South Carolina,
by the University of South Carolina Press, 2011

www.sc.edu/uscpress

Manufactured in the United States of America

20 19 18 17 16 15 14 13 12 11   10 9 8 7 6 5 4 3 2 1

Grateful acknowledgment is given to New Directions Publishing Corporation
for U.S./Canadian permission to quote from the following copyrighted works
of Tennessee Williams:

"Portrait of a Girl in Glass" © 1948 by Tennessee Williams. "Three Players
of a Summer Game" © 1952 by Tennessee Williams. "The Man in the Over-
stuffed Chair" © 1980 by Tennessee Williams. "The Night of the Iguana"
© 1948 by Tennessee Williams. In *Collected Stories:* © 1985 by The Estate of
Tennessee Williams. *In the Winter of Cities:* © 1956, 1964, by Tennessee Williams. *The Glass Menagerie:* © 1945 by Tennessee Williams. *A Streetcar Named
Desire:* © 1947 by Tennessee Williams. *Summer and Smoke:* © 1948 by Tennessee Williams. *The Rose Tattoo:* © 1950 by Tennessee Williams. *Camino Real:*
As "Ten Blocks on the Camino Real" (a one-act play), © 1948 by Tennessee
Williams. As "Camino Real," revised and published version, © 1953 by Tennessee Williams. *Cat on a Hot Tin Roof:* © 1954, 1955, by Tennessee Williams.
Orpheus Descending: © 1955, 1958, by Tennessee Williams. *Sweet Bird of
Youth:* © 1959 by Two Rivers Enterprises, Inc. *The Night of the Iguana:* © 1961
by Two Rivers Enterprises, Inc. *The Milk Train Doesn't Stop Here Anymore:*
© 1976 by Tennessee Williams. *Where I Live:* © 1944, 1945, 1947, 1948, 1950,
1951, 1952, 1953, 1957, 1958, 1960, 1961, 1963, 1972, 1973, 1978, by Tennessee Williams.

Grateful acknowledgment is given to The Lady Maria St. Just and John
Eastman, Esq., cotrustees under the will of Tennessee Williams, for permission
to quote in all other territories.

**Library of Congress Cataloging-in-Publication Data
will be found at the end of this book.**

ISBN: 978-1-61117-006-1 (pbk)

For John A. and John B.

CONTENTS

EDITOR'S PREFACE

The volumes of *Understanding Contemporary American Literature* have been planned as guides or companions for students as well as good nonacademic readers. The editor and publisher perceive a need for these volumes because much of the influential contemporary literature makes special demands. Uninitiated readers encounter difficulty in approaching works that depart from the traditional forms and techniques of prose and poetry. Literature relies on conventions, but the conventions keep evolving; new writers form their own conventions—which in time may become familiar. Put simply, *UCAL* provides instruction in how to read certain contemporary writers—identifying and explicating their material, themes, use of language, point of view, structures, symbolism, and responses to experience.

The word *understanding* in the titles was deliberately chosen. Many willing readers lack an adequate understanding of how contemporary literature works; that is, what the author is attempting to express and the means by which it is conveyed. Although the criticism and analysis in the series have been aimed at a level of general accessibility, these introductory volumes are meant to be applied in conjunction with the works they cover. They do not provide a substitute for the works and authors they introduce, but rather prepare the reader for more profitable literary experiences.

M. J. B.

PREFACE

This book is offered as a guide to Tennessee Williams's major plays for those who read them, those who view them, and those who stage them. Although there exists an extensive bibliography, there is surprisingly little in-depth evaluation of the nine plays that established Williams as America's greatest lyric playwright. Some studies regard Williams primarily as a literary figure, others as a stage innovator, but a comprehensive consideration must explore both aspects, as does this book.

Analyzing language, characters, themes, dramatic effects, and staging, this study also calls attention to Williams's unique gift for heightened dialogue, which is convincing as speech and at the same time poetic. Realizing that his new approach to drama required a new style of staging, Williams rebelled against the prevailing realism that had dominated the American theater for over forty years. Insisting that his plays were "not realistic," he called for a "plastic" presentation, an artistic unity in which action, characters, dialogue, setting, and stage effects all combined to express the theme. But revolution came slowly to the commercial theater; only recently have Williams's aims in staging been fully realized.

As a theater editor and critic as well as a university teacher during the period in which the works here considered were first produced on Broadway, I was in a position not only to view the plays as originally staged but also to

PREFACE

discuss them with Williams and his directors and actors. Later scholars who have depended on the first reviews, conveniently collected and published as *New York Theatre Critics' Reviews,* have failed to recognize (as did the reviewers) that, when Williams aimed for one kind of production, he often received another, widely divergent from his stated intentions. When Blanche in *Streetcar* was viewed as a "boozy prostitute" by a reviewer, the first academic study in 1961 (and still on the shelves of many public libraries) not only quoted the review but adopted its viewpoint. To remedy such secondhand judgments and their influence upon subsequent considerations of the plays, included here are observations on the original stage presentations and examinations of their validity when measured against Williams's stated aims.

In keeping with the editorial goals of this series, the nine major plays are considered in depth, each as an artistic entity to which a chapter is devoted. Later full-length plays and significant earlier one-acts are mentioned in the introductory chapter, while short stories and poems, where relevant, are referred to in discussions of the plays. An annotated bibliography is provided for further study.

Because the nine major plays are so popular, their published texts are numerous, both in single volumes and in collections—seven, for instance, of *The Glass Menagerie* alone. While most libraries should have the eight-volume standard edition of the collected plays, *The Theatre*

PREFACE

of Tennessee Williams, published by New Directions, most high school and college courses are using paperbacks, the Signet New American Library in single volumes or collected as *Three by Tennessee* and *Four by Tennessee.* In the United Kingdom and Canada the plays are issued in paperback by Penguin. Other publishers also have produced Williams's plays singly and in collections. Because of the variety of printed texts, quotations are referred to by act and/or scene instead of by page numbers. The ellipses that Williams uses to designate pauses are identified as his in the quoted text. All others are mine.

ACKNOWLEDGMENTS

As this volume evolved from the spoken word—my radio reviews immediately following the plays' Broadway openings and later discussions in graduate seminars I conducted on Tennessee Williams—I owe my thanks to stations WNYC and WBAI in New York for accommodating broadcasts at unusual hours and to the students at Lehman (formerly Hunter) College for sessions that were always lively and perceptive. I appreciate as well the helpful advice and assistance from friends and colleagues, including Alice Boatwright, Robert Ganshaw, Harry Goldman, Barbara Guiffre, Austin Pendleton, and Katharine Worth. The staffs of the Theater Collection of the New York Public Library, Columbia University Library, and the British Library are to be commended for their work in complying with my requests for material that required special searches. For their efforts in behalf of this volume I thank University of South Carolina Press editor Kenneth Scott and his staff.

My greatest debt of gratitude goes jointly to my partner in marriage and in drama criticism, John B., and to our son, John A., for sharing my enthusiasm and encouraging my research. It is to them, with love, that this volume is dedicated.

UNDERSTANDING
TENNESSEE WILLIAMS

CHAPTER ONE

Understanding Tennessee Williams

Career

Thomas Lanier Williams was born on 26 March 1911, in the Episcopal rectory of Columbus, Mississippi, home of his maternal grandfather. His father, Cornelius Coffin Williams, was descended from "pioneer Tennessee stock," hence the writer's adopted first name. In 1918 the family moved to St. Louis, when his father, a traveling salesman for a shoe company, was promoted to the firm's headquarters there. Because of their Southern speech and manners, Tom and his older sister Rose, who had enjoyed a happy childhood, now became the butt of schoolmates' jokes. For the first time they realized they "were economically less fortunate than others." The family of five (his brother Dakin was born the next year) lived in a small apartment amid "ugly rows of apartment buildings the color of dried blood and mustard." [1]

In junior high and high school Williams wrote poems and stories and at the age of sixteen won a prize from *Smart Set* magazine for his essay "Can a Good Wife Be a Good Sport?" He answered in the negative, assuming the role of a traveling salesman whose wife misbehaved in his absence. A year later his first short story was published in

Weird Tales. His relations with his father were always difficult: "He was not a man capable of examining his behavior toward his family, or not capable of changing it. My mother devoted herself to us three kids and developed an hostility toward him, which he took out on me, the first male to replace him. He thought me, which I certainly was, a terrible sissy, and used to call me 'Miss Nancy' . . . because I wouldn't play baseball with the other boys and preferred girl playmates."[2] At eleven Williams began a close childhood friendship, which ripened into love, with a neighbor, Hazel Kramer, "the greatest extrafamilial love of my life."[3] He and Hazel were to part when his father insisted they not attend the same college.

Williams entered the University of Missouri in 1929, but in his third year, when he failed ROTC, his father refused to pay the tuition, and Williams returned home to work as a warehouse clerk for the International Shoe Company at sixty-five dollars a month. Working days and writing at night, he became exhausted and suffered a breakdown. He recuperated in Memphis at the home of his Dakin grandparents, now retired from the ministry. Here he co-authored his first play, *Cairo! Shanghai! Bombay!* staged by an amateur group in 1935. He returned to St. Louis to finish college at Washington University but transferred to the University of Iowa in 1937 to study play writing and received his B.A. degree in English in 1938. While he was away, without his knowledge, his parents gave consent for his sister Rose to have a prefrontal lobotomy to cure her schizophrenia, which had grown steadily more acute. The operation was not a success; she remained institutionalized for the rest of her days, outliving her brother, whose guilt and whose love for his sister remained constant, as reflected in much of his writing, especially *The Glass Menagerie.*

After graduation Williams wandered about the country for a year, applied to the Work Projects Administration (WPA) writers' project in Chicago but was refused and traveled to New Orleans, where he had his first homosexual experience. In 1939, in an act that would change his life, he entered four of his one-act plays in a contest sponsored by the Group Theater in New York. The letter informing him of his hundred-dollar prize was signed by Harold Clurman, Theresa Helburn, and Molly Day Thacher (later Mrs. Elia Kazan). Audrey Wood became Williams's agent and secured for him a $1,000 grant from the Rockefeller Foundation.

With the money Williams went to New York to study advanced play writing with John Gassner and Erwin Piscator at the New School for Social Research. Gassner recommended that the Theater Guild produce Williams's play *Battle of Angels,* which opened in Boston at the end of 1940 with Miriam Hopkins in the leading role of Myra. Williams recalls, "The play was pretty far out for its time and included, among other tactical errors, a mixture of superreligiosity and hysterical sexuality coexisting in a central character. The critics and police censors seemed to regard this play as a theatrical counterpart of the bubonic plague surfacing in their city." [4] The play quickly closed, and Williams began revising it in Key West, Florida. Seventeen years later it emerged as *Orpheus Descending.* In the military draft for World War II Williams received a 4F rating because of his bad health and supported himself during those years in various jobs, including waiter, teletype operator, cashier, and movie usher. He continued writing "not with any hope of making a living at it but because [he] found no other means of expressing things that seemed to demand expression": "There was never a moment when I did not find life to be immeasurably exciting to experience and to witness, however difficult it was to sustain." [5]

But, having been a professional playwright, even though briefly, he was offered a six-month contract by MGM Studios at $250 a week to write a movie for Lana Turner. The studio turned down his film script and asked him to write one for Margaret O'Brien; he declined and proposed instead, as a new *Gone with the Wind,* a mammoth Southern epic, which was an early projection of *A Streetcar Named Desire.* MGM refused the proposal and also rejected his screenplay called *The Gentleman Caller,* which would become *The Glass Menagerie.* Then the studio dismissed Williams, but his pay continued until the contract expired, during which time he completed *The Glass Menagerie.*

UNDERSTANDING TENNESSEE WILLIAMS

Once it opened on Broadway in March 1945, Williams's place in the American theater was assured.

In the next sixteen years all of the major plays would be produced, Williams would receive prizes, including Pulitzers, awards, honorary degrees, and invitations to membership in prestigious organizations. He published short stories, one-act plays, poetry, and a novel. Each of the major plays as well as one of the one-acts (*This Property Is Condemned*) was made into a motion picture.

In 1956 Williams's frank, outspoken film *Baby Doll* opened, to be blasted by the critics and condemned by New York's Cardinal Spellman. Twenty-seven of Williams's one-act plays have been published, including the two from which the film was derived, *Twenty-Seven Wagons Full of Cotton,* concerning a brutal Southern cotton-gin operator, his nubile wife, and a Latin visitor; and *The Unsatisfactory Supper,* portraying the trials of a birdlike spinster aunt who cooks for the household. Other outstanding one-acts written in the 1940s include: *The Purification,* a verse tragedy in the style of García Lorca; *This Property Is Condemned,* a monologue by a pathetic Southern waif; *The Last of My Solid Gold Watches,* about a lonely traveling salesman at the end of his career; *Portrait of a Madonna,* about a faded Southern belle whose remembrance of lost love in times past ends with a trip to the sanitorium; *The Long Goodbye,* a young man's reverie about his mother and sister as movers empty their apartment; and *Lord Byron's Love*

Letters, which became the libretto for an opera about an aging woman with romantic memories of an affair with Byron. These one-acts reveal Williams's skill at creating an artistic unity of characters, dialogue, and mood. The narrative line is slight, the exposition expertly handled, and the poetic monologues prefigure the long "arias" of the major plays, which premiered on Broadway from 1945 to 1961.

In 1958 the short play *Suddenly Last Summer* opened off Broadway; the good reviews surprised Williams, who confessed that he had expected to be run out of town on a rail; he regretted that the film version with Katharine Hepburn turned "a short morality play, in a lyrical style . . . into a sensationally successful film that the public thinks was a literal study of such things as cannibalism, madness, and sexual deviation."[6] (An excellent television version directed by Richard Eyre appeared in 1992.) In 1960 Williams's second comedy, *Period of Adjustment,* opened to favorable reviews. It concerns two couples; the pair on their honeymoon, a sexually timid woman and an impotent man, arrive on Christmas eve to visit the man's former buddy, who is in the midst of a domestic imbroglio. Williams's humor is delightful, the farce fast-moving, and, even though minor Williams, the characterization, dialogue, and symbolism bear his unmistakable mark. The 1962 film with Jane Fonda and Tony Franciosa preserves most of the action as well as the original ending, a happy one, which therefore did not undergo the usual Hollywood transformation of Williams's conclusions.

UNDERSTANDING TENNESSEE WILLIAMS

A fourteen-year intimacy with Frank Merlo began in 1948, and, when Merlo died of cancer in the 1960s, Williams endured depression, turned to alcohol and drugs, and spent three months in a mental institution. He refers to this period as his "Stoned Age." Although he continued to write every day, the plays from this period are minor ones. The least of them is interesting, for Williams never lost what he termed his "seventh sense" of theater, and three of the best ones, had they not been compared with his earlier works, might have been received more generously. They are *Small Craft Warnings, Out Cry (The Two-Character Play),* and *Clothes for a Summer Hotel.*

The Milk Train Doesn't Stop Here Anymore was produced on Broadway in 1963, with Hermione Baddeley as the aged, temperamental Flora Goforth at whose Capri villa arrives a handsome young poet, Chris. His nickname is "Angel of Death" because his visits to ill older women always seem to culminate in their deaths. Although the action is erratic and the Kabuki-style scene changes disruptive, there is an elegiac mood created and sustained. The play concerns death and its acceptance, a motif introduced by the old poet Jonathan Coffin in *The Night of the Iguana,* now developed into a main theme in which the knell, or "boom," of the waves sounds continually. Some of the writing has the indelible Williams stamp, like Chris's speech in scene 5 about the two sleeping pets huddled together, whose "owner's house is never a sure protection, a reliable shelter. . . . We're all of us living in a house we're

not used to. . . .we try to— be—*pleasingly playful* . . . but—
in our hearts, we're all very frightened." The character of
Flora is obviously autobiographical, as are central characters in succeeding plays.

It would seem that the more autobiographical Williams's
later work became, the more he lost the fine artistic disci-
pline and control that mark the major plays. After a very
brief, unsuccessful run, *Milk Train* was revived with Tallulah
Bankhead as Flora and made into a film in 1968 as *Boom!*
with Elizabeth Taylor and Richard Burton, directed by
Joseph Losey.

In 1966 Broadway saw the production of *Slapstick
Tragedy*, a double bill of one-acts, including *The Gnädiges
Fräulein* and *The Mutilated*. The latter concerns two women,
both "mutilated," one by a mastectomy and the other by her
wretched state, having just been released from jail. Each
woman, despite berating the other, realizes their mutual
dependency. The former, more weighty play, is satiric,
expressionistic, farcical, and fantastic, with Margaret
Leighton creating the title role of a once famous star, now
a derelict, wearing her old finery, fighting the Cocaloony
birds for fish, with which she pays for her lodging in the
broken-down rooming house that is the setting. As the
action progresses, she becomes increasingly mutilated by
the Cocaloony, finally losing her eyes. Viewing the work as
an allegory concerning Williams (the Fräulein), his com-
petitors (the birds), and success (the fish), critic Harold

Clurman declared it "an odd but effective mixture of gallows humor and Rabelaisian zest": "Though I was able to appreciate the style I could not bring myself to smile. I was too conscious that its author was in pain."[7]

The Seven Descents of Myrtle (Kingdom of Earth) opened on Broadway in 1968 to unfavorable reviews. Reminiscent of O'Neill's *Desire under the Elms,* but lacking its power and structure, the work concerns two brothers, Lot and Chicken. The effete, dying Lot marries Myrtle on a television show and brings her home, to prevent the earthy Chicken, who is illegitimate and half-black, from inheriting their farm. Lot succumbs, the floodwaters are rising, and the practical Myrtle realizes that her survival depends upon Chicken.

Small Craft Warnings was performed off-Broadway in 1972, an expanded version of an earlier short work, *Confessional,* in which each of the characters at various times leaves the action, advances downstage, and, spotlit, reveals, as if in a confession box, his or her innermost thoughts. The title refers literally to the marine warnings given small boats when rough weather is anticipated and, symbolically, to the collection of drifters and misfits who congregate nightly in a run-down beachfront bar. Another symbol of their plight is a mounted sailfish, once king of the sea but now worthless, dangling crazily as a ceiling decoration. The most lively customer is Leona, a tough, optimistic hairdresser. She has been sharing her mobile home with, but is about to dispossess, a stud who welcomes the advances of Violet, a weepy prostitute whose weakness contrasts with Leona's strength. When the actor playing Doc fell ill, Williams himself played the role of a has-been who performs illegal operations. The work is neither as optimistic as Saroyan's *The Time of Your Life* nor as pessimistic as O'Neill's *The Iceman Cometh,* both of which it resembles. Good characterization, lively dialogue, and the presence of Williams (who from the stage participated in postperformance discussions) contributed to the deserved success of *Small Craft Warnings.* In 1975 Williams's autobiography *Memoirs* and his autobiographical novel *Moise and the World of Reason* both appeared.

Another important Williams play, *Out Cry,* was presented on Broadway in 1973, with Michael York and Cara Duff-MacCormick as two actors, a brother and sister who find themselves locked in a theater, deserted by their touring company, with no scenery or audience; nevertheless, they proceed to enact their roles in the play-within-the-play. It concerns a tragedy in their own earlier lives in a Southern town. Poetic and free in its form, moving between the actors' lonely, fearful plight in the empty theater and their enactment of assigned roles in a scheduled play, the work was interpreted as autobiographical. In the *New York Times* of 2 May 1971 Williams describes the play's earlier version, *The Two-Character Play,* as "a tragedy with laughter": "It affirms nothing but gallantry in the face of defeat."

UNDERSTANDING TENNESSEE WILLIAMS

Two lesser plays opened in 1976 and 1977. *The Red Devil Battery Sign,* which played briefly in Boston, viewed international big business, rather than society (as in earlier plays), as a destructive force. Intent on war, the Red Devil cartel will not be deterred by the weak idealists who oppose it, mambo musician King Del Ray (Anthony Quinn) and his Woman Downtown (Claire Bloom). In *Vieux Carré* on Broadway Sylvia Sidney played the domineering landlady Mrs. Wire in Williams's recreation of his early boarding-house days in New Orleans. The inhabitants include a dying homosexual, two malnourished gentlewomen, a male hustler, and a once fashionable lady. The reviews of both plays were markedly unfavorable.

Another more appealing minor work, *A Lovely Sunday for Creve Coeur,* was presented on Broadway in 1979, set in St. Louis in the mid-1930s, with Shirley Knight as the delicate, Blanche-like high school teacher. Her practical German roommate, Bodey, steers Dorothea away from a hopeless liaison with the principal and into a day out with Bodey and her admiring, though stodgy, brother at the amusement park Creve Coeur.

Clothes for a Summer Hotel, Williams's last full-length play to be staged on Broadway in his lifetime, opened in 1980 on his sixty-ninth birthday. The "summer hotel" is the mental institution in which Zelda Fitzgerald burned to death when the frame building was engulfed by fire and the confined patients could not flee. The central incident is a visit to his wife by F. Scott Fitzgerald, still wearing his Hollywood "summer clothes." Events move back and forth in time, detailing a brief affair of Zelda's, Scott's relationship with Ernest Hemingway, and the conflict between Zelda and Scott, whom she accuses of stifling her talent and stealing her life to create his successful novels. Some saw in this an analogy to Williams and his sister Rose. Although the structure may be sketchy and a knowledge of the Fitzgeralds' personal life is helpful, some of the dialogue is among Williams's best, and the mounting intensity highly dramatic, especially so because of Zelda's actual end.

Like Mark Antony's favoring god deserting him before the decisive battle, Williams's fortunes were against him on opening night. Although the leading roles were well played by Geraldine Page and Kenneth Haigh, the acoustical system at the Cort Theater developed a fault, causing a distraction, which seemed in part responsible for the unfavorable reviews from critics unable or unwilling to distinguish between the play and its production.

Alone in a hotel room in New York Williams died three years later, having choked to death on the cap of an eye medicine bottle removed by and held in his teeth while leaning back to apply drops to his ever-ailing eyes. He had continued writing to the end, appending to his drafts the battle cry "En Avant," struggling with bad health and his "blue devil," despairing over bad reviews. In 1970, in his prose poem read at a London poetry festival, Williams seems to anticipate his end: "not yet again, not so far . . . the very deep toe-curling stabs of a black-coated assassin's stiletto, that fierce opponent of your fierce will to continue, no, not that again, not so far, that long, long moment of air-starvation and anguish." [8]

David Mamet's eulogy recounted Williams's impact on theater in the years of the major plays, and then, as "his life and view of life became less immediately accessible, our gratitude was changed to distant reverence for a man whom we felt obliged—if we were to continue in our happy feelings toward him—to consider already dead." The irony was apparent to Mamet, who observes that Americans are "a kind people living in a cruel country": "We don't know how to show our love. This was the subject of his plays, the greatest dramatic poetry in the American language. We thank him and we wish him, with love, the best we could have done and did not. We wish him what he wished us: the peace that we all are seeking." [9]

Art and Dramatic Theory

When David Mamet describes Williams's plays as "the greatest dramatic poetry in the American language," he expresses the generally held opinion that Williams brought to the language of the American theater a lyricism un-equaled before or after. Williams did not write "poetic plays," such as Maxwell Anderson had attempted earlier, with limited appeal and success. Rather, as Mamet notes, Williams's plays are "dramatic poetry." He infuses his dialogue with lyrical qualities so subtle that the reader or hearer, unaware, responds not to realistic speech but, instead, to speech heightened by such poetic effects as alliteration, rhythm, onomatopoeia, and assonance. As a Southern writer, Williams was attuned to the natural rhythm and melody of Southern speech, a melody, he says, heard especially in the voices of women. Critic Stark Young, himself a Southerner, heard in *The Glass Menagerie* "behind the Southern speech in the mother's part . . . the echo of great literature, or at least respect for it." [10]

In addition to imperceptibly heightening the dialogue of his characters, Williams uses their speech to emphasize their individuality. Amanda in *The Glass Menagerie* is loquacious through desperation; Vee's dialogue in *Orpheus Descending* is "breathless," as much a sign of her sexual frustration as are her paintings. Alma's dedication to the spirit in the first part of *Summer and Smoke* is reflected in her airy speech about the Gulf Wind. Williams's unlettered people have as much poetry—of their own kind—in their dialogue as do those better educated. Stanley Kowalski in *Streetcar* has his unique rhythms, based on repetition and inflection; Serafina in *The Rose Tattoo* displays eloquence in monosyllables; Val in *Orpheus Descending* has a speech about a little bird which is at the same time lyric, soaring, and, as befits the character, simple yet touched by strangeness.

UNDERSTANDING TENNESSEE WILLIAMS

Characterization is one of Williams's strongest achievements as a dramatist. His people are imaginatively conceived yet so convincing that it is tempting to take them out of context (as does one handbook) and theorize about their lives before and after the action of the play. Amanda and Laura, Blanche and Stanley, Alma and John, Hannah and Shannon—each is memorable not only as an individual but also in his or her contrasting relationship with the other. Often the protagonist is an outsider, misunderstood and suspect by the community, like Val in *Orpheus* and Kilroy in *Camino Real*.

Frequently, Williams will view his major characters as fugitives, desperately fleeing a stalker, perhaps Time or Death, who has almost caught up. As these men and women pause for a visit during their flights, they face their adversaries with spirit and gallantry, even though defeat may be imminent and inevitable. They may be seeking protection when despair threatens or struggling at the end of their tether like the iguana. But, despite the critics who narrowly view Williams as morbid and pessimistic, there is optimism and hope in his plays. His compassion for his characters is boundless; there are few out-and-out villains— perhaps only Jabe Torrance, who is after all the Prince of Darkness, in *Orpheus*. Williams said, "I don't believe in villains or heroes—only right or wrong ways that individuals have taken, not by choice but by necessity or by certain still-uncomprehended influences in themselves, their circumstances, and their antecedents." [11]

In place of realism, which stressed photographic duplication of the actual, a style that had dominated the American stage for four decades, Williams insisted on a theater that was "plastic," that combined all the elements of production—dialogue, action, setting, lighting, even properties—in a unified, symbolic expression of a truth. This approach, revolutionary for its time, he explains in his introduction to *The Glass Menagerie* and demonstrates its validity by the play itself. Ironically, throughout his career Williams was praised for his "realism" by critics such as Eric Bentley, who recognized little else of value in his work. Such critics may have been fooled into categorizing Williams as realistic because he grounds his poetic dialogue in such concrete details as proper names, specific locales and references, popular songs, and catchphrases of the day. The fact that the original production of *Menagerie* and of his subsequent major plays fell far short of Williams's desire for a plastic presentation led to misunderstanding and even attacks on his method by many of the early critics, from whom some later scholars took their cue. But Williams's sheer dramatic urgency, together with enthusiastic audience response, assured the works of their success. As theater production in the 1980s and 1990s developed in the direction Williams pioneered on the commercial stage, some major revivals of his works have achieved the presentation he sought.

Another important contribution Williams made to the stage of his day was in airing subjects formerly considered

UNDERSTANDING TENNESSEE WILLIAMS

taboo, including homosexuality, nymphomania, and rape, all denounced in *A Streetcar Named Desire* by critics who viewed the work as "obscene," "a sewer," and "a cesspool." Failing to recognize the lyricism and symbolism of the plays, most of the early critics saw only the subject matter, which they frequently found shocking. Williams defended the "unlocking and lighting up and ventilation of the closets, attics, and basements of human behavior and experience" as an advance in modern theater and insisted that "no significant area of human experience, and behavior reaction to it, should be held inaccessible, provided it is presented with honest intention and taste." [12]

Williams's themes are universal, and his structure is frequently that of a visit by his protagonist to a microcosm of the world itself. Their fears are common ones—the tyranny of time and of death, which might be transcended by love and procreation, the loss of youth and beauty, loneliness: "sentenced to solitary confinement in our own skins." Reflecting the exploitation of the sensitive and weak by the crude and strong, *A Streetcar Named Desire* illustrates these themes. The streetcars named Desire and Cemetery symbolize the opposition and conjunction of death and desire. Other themes also treat contrasts: between flesh and spirit (*Summer and Smoke*), between the heroic past and the realistic present (*Camino Real*), between responsibility and desertion (*The Glass Menagerie*), between deception and truth (*Cat on a Hot Tin Roof*). *The Night of the Iguana* illuminates the "humble nobility" of two desperate people whose salvation lies in putting concern for the other above that for oneself. Often the theme is symbolized by an everyday image expressed in the title, like *The Rose Tattoo.*

"Some critics resent my symbols, but let me ask, what would I do without them? Without my symbols I might still be employed by the International Shoe Company in St. Louis," comments Williams humorously.[13] In Williams's concept of a plastic theater symbolism expressing the theme is integral to the characters, action, setting, costumes, properties, and sound as well as to the dialogue itself. In a realistic play such as *Detective Story* a clock is important because time passing increases the dramatic tension. With Williams a clock is never just a clock. In *Sweet Bird of Youth,* in which the title itself, as well as the characters, deplores the passing of time and the flight of youth, a clock is heard ticking in the play's final moments. Chance (his name, like that of many Williams characters, is symbolic) remarks: "I didn't know there was a clock in this room," to which the Princess replies, "I guess there's a clock in every room people live in."

That Williams's plays are as fresh and relevant today as when they first appeared is a tribute to his genius, about which he was genuinely modest. Charged with writing only about his own life, Williams defended his approach: "It is the responsibility of the writer to put his experience as a being into work that refines it and elevates it and that makes of it an essence that a wide audience can somehow manage to feel in themselves: 'This is true.'" [14] When he died in 1983 alone in a hotel room, deserted by former friends, dependent on "the kindness of strangers," his legacy was priceless: nine great stage works whose lyricism, humanity, and theatrical impact enriched the achievement of the American theater and the hearts of its audience. Williams's comment on Proust's *Remembrance of Things Past* might well express his own epitaph, giving to the theater plays which contain "his love, fear, loneliness, disgust, humor, and most important of all, his forgiving perception of the reasons for the tragicomedy of human confusion." [15]

Notes

1. Tennessee Williams, "Facts about Me," *Where I Live: Selected Essays,* ed. Christine R. Day and Bob Woods (New York: New Directions, 1978), 58–60.

2. Tennessee Williams, *Letters to Donald Windham, 1940–1965,* ed. Donald Windham (New York: Holt, Rinehart and Winston, 1976), 302.

3. Tennessee Williams, *Memoirs* (Garden City, N.Y.: Doubleday, 1975), 15.

4. Ibid., 62.

5. Williams, "Facts about Me," 61–62.

6. Williams, "Five Fiery Ladies," *Where I Live,* 130–31.

7. Harold Clurman, "Theater," *Nation* 202, 14 March 1966, 309.

8. Tennessee Williams, "What's Next on the Agenda, Mr. Williams?" in *Five O'Clock Angel: Letters of Tennessee Williams to Maria St. Just, 1948–1982,* ed. Maria St. Just (New York: Alfred A. Knopf, 1990), 204–5.

9. David Mamet, "Tennessee Williams," *Rolling Stone,* 14 April 1983, 124.

10. Stark Young, "The Glass Menagerie," *New Republic* 112, 16 April 1945, 505.

11. "Tennessee Williams Interviews Himself," *Where I Live,* 91–92.

12. "Tennessee Williams Presents His POV," *Where I Live,* 116–17.

13. Williams, "A Summer of Discovery," *Where I Live,* 142.

14. Williams, "Too Personal?" *Where I Live,* 159.

15. Williams, "Prelude to a Comedy," *Where I Live,* 125.

CHAPTER TWO

The Glass Menagerie

The curtain first rose on *The Glass Menagerie* in December 1944 in Chicago, and by March of the following year, when it opened on Broadway, Williams was being hailed as a welcome new voice in the American theater. Rosamond Gilder rejoiced in *Theatre Arts* magazine that "just as the 1944–45 season, pushed into the wings by mighty public events, was about to subside into featureless anonymity, a minor miracle took place": "In the middle of routine productions . . . the theater suddenly asserted itself in its own best terms. Tennessee Williams's *The Glass Menagerie* proved once again what magic can be wrought. . . . [I]t has a significance and abundance of life, a variety and complexity, that is the hallmark of creative achievement.[1]

Since then it has become his most popular play, performed on stages all over the world, a staple of high school and college literature courses. With a lyricism new to the American stage and a theatricalism that would define his future works, Williams in *The Glass Menagerie* dramatizes responsibility and guilt in the family relationship and examines the question at its core: "Am I my brother's / sister's keeper?"

With humor, grace, and compassion Williams looks back at his own family and through his unique alchemy transforms a single incident—the visit of a dinner guest—

into a universal revelation about parent-child conflict and brother-sister bonding. The visit, casual for the guest, assumes near tragic proportions for the mother and sister.

To express his universal truths Williams created what he termed plastic theater, a distinctive new style of drama. He insisted that setting, properties, music, sound, and visual effects—all the elements of staging—must combine to reflect and enhance the action, theme, characters, and language. The result is an artistic entity that Williams describes as "lyric" and "dynamic."

From *The Glass Menagerie,* with its final stage picture that haunts not only Tom but audiences as well, through *The Night of the Iguana,* with its celebration of compassion in an Eden-like setting, Williams displays his new type of theater. As he states in his "Production Notes," he seeks to break the constraints of the "exhausted" realistic plays of his day and to employ "poetic imagination" to represent "truth, life, or reality" through "transformation."

Transforming reality through stage magic begins with the son Tom's opening words: "Yes, I have tricks in my pocket, I have things up my sleeve. But I am the opposite of a stage magician. He gives you illusion that has the appearance of truth. I give you truth in the pleasant disguise of illusion." Here Williams also gives the audience poetry in the pleasant disguise of ordinary speech. The poetic devices of these opening lines—balance and antithesis, alliteration, repetition and rhythm—were new to conversa-

THE GLASS MENAGERIE

tional stage dialogue and were to characterize Williams's work to come. Symbolism and word play abound, like the telephone idiom Tom uses to describe his long-absent father: "a telephone man who fell in love with long distances. . . . The last we heard of him was a picture postcard . . . containing a message of two words: 'Hello—Goodbye!'"

Tom (Williams's first name was Thomas) introduces the other characters in the play, his mother, Amanda, his sister, Laura, and a gentleman caller, "the most realistic character in the play, being an emissary from a world of reality that we were somehow set apart from."

Amanda Wingfield is the first in a line of memorable women Williams will create, and, like the others, she is a many-faceted, unique individual. But Amanda is also a universal type, a mother with the characteristic qualities of devotion to her offspring and determination to survive for their sakes. She is, however, an extremist who carries these traits to their limits, and beyond. She may, like all mothers, nag Tom to eat more and Laura to do her homework, but only Amanda can chirp so cheerfully each morning, "Rise and shine!" to her weary son or urge him, in scene 1, "chew—chew! Animals have secretions in their stomachs which enable them to digest food without mastication, but human beings are supposed to chew their food before they swallow it down."

Although the family now lives in reduced circumstances in St. Louis on Tom's salary of sixty-five dollars a month as a warehouse clerk, Amanda never stops reminding her children of her own more affluent past. Reminiscing is a recognizable parental characteristic, but it is an obsession with Amanda. In his introduction to "The Characters" Williams says she is "clinging frantically to another time and place."

Retreating from the harsh reality of the Depression to the illusion of herself in the legendary Old South of elegant beaux and belles makes the present somehow more bearable for Amanda. Laura understands this, as she begs Tom, impatient with his mother's oft-told tale, to "let her tell it. . . . She loves to tell it," as Amanda in scene 1 launches into the first of her arias about the past: "One Sunday afternoon in Blue Mountain—your mother received—*seventeen!*— gentlemen callers! . . . My callers were gentlemen—all! Among my callers were some of the most prominent young planters of the Mississippi Delta—planters and sons of planters!" The myth of the Old South, in which Amanda devoutly believes, was one of gracious living, family tradition, chivalry, and coquetry which lent a stability of time and place to those who partook of it, as Thomas E. Porter points out. Alienation from place led to the "preoccupation with time" which affects Amanda as she constantly harks back to earlier days.[2]

Strangely anachronistic in a 1930s tenement, Amanda's airs and graces are those of a woman brought up only to look attractive, behave graciously, and choose a husband from among many suitors. Although in her recollections she is sought after by many eligible young men (ironically, she tells Tom that "character" is important in choosing a mate), these happy courting days ended sadly. Unfortunately, her upbringing did not prepare her to choose a mate for qualities other than "charm," nor did it train her to earn her own living when her charming spouse deserted her. To supplement Tom's meager salary she has demonstrated brassieres at a department store for the fifty dollars' tuition for Laura at business school and now sells magazine subscriptions by phone to decorate the apartment for the expected dinner guest.

Despite her lapses into her earlier, more glorious days, Amanda does not live in the past—a luxury she could not afford. She recognizes that their situation is near desperate, but she is unable to accept Tom and Laura as they are. Laura is crippled, though Amanda insists on never allowing "that word to be used!" Tom, who hates his warehouse job, wants only to be left alone to write, but Amanda refuses to recognize or accept his creative work or even the books he reads: "That hideous book by that insane Mr. Lawrence. . . . I cannot control the output of diseased minds. . . . BUT I WON'T ALLOW SUCH FILTH BROUGHT INTO MY HOUSE!" (sc. 3). Tom's escape is to go to the movies, a pastime Amanda resents. As Williams introduces Amanda in "The Characters," he notes that "there is much to admire in Amanda, and as much to love and pity as there is to laugh at. Certainly she has endurance and a kind of heroism, and though her foolishness makes her unwittingly cruel at times, there is tenderness in her slight person."

Delma Presley sees Amanda, along with Laura and even Jim, as "characters caught up in illusions of their own making": "All of them . . . have built their lives on insubstantial premises of deception." And it is Amanda "who always seems to reap the bitter consequences of deception," by her husband, by Laura (in going to the zoo instead of business school), by Tom (in using the light bill money to join the merchant seamen), and even, unwittingly, by the gentleman caller.[3] One must keep in mind, however, that Amanda, despite her urging "gay deceivers" (bosom enhancers) upon Laura in scene 6, deceives no one except perhaps herself, for she really believes in her role as a Southern belle.

The visual image and its implications were as important to Williams as his dialogue: "When I write, everything is visual, as brilliantly as if it were on a lit stage."[4] In scene 6 Amanda becomes a touching visual image of the futility of attempting to recreate the past in the present. Although she is now twice the age of the belle she was, she dons for the invited gentleman caller a "girlish frock of yellowed voile with a blue silk sash," which she found in an old trunk, wears her hair in ringlets, and carries a bunch of jonquils to revive the "legend of her youth . . . nearly." With dinner guest Jim, as if he were her suitor, she behaves with "girlish

Southern vivacity . . . social charm. . . . gay laughter and chatter." The vignette is as gently humorous as it is pathetic.

As he will do with his future heroines, Williams gives Amanda a distinctive idiom. Her two long speeches to Jim in scene 6 are characteristic: "I've heard so much about you from my boy. I finally said to him, Tom—good gracious!— why don't you bring this paragon to supper? I'd like to meet this nice young man at the warehouse!—instead of just hearing him sing your praises so much! I don't know why my son is so stand-offish—that's not Southern behavior!" (Southern behavior in Amanda's view evidently did not value facts as much as style.) After one word from Jim and four from Tom, she expands on her "gracious living. . . . gentlemen callers . . . sons of planters" and marriage to a man who "travels and I don't even know where!" She is breathlessly loquacious, as if endless talking could stave off an unexpected Caller, who might just be gentlemanly enough to wait until she has finished.

Because most of his heroines are Southern, Williams can heighten what he observes to be the "natural elo-quence" of Southern women. In Amanda's speeches critic Stark Young hears "the echo of great literature." [5] Fearing Laura will be a spinster, Amanda in scene 2 onomatopoeti-cally describes such women as "little birdlike women without any nest—eating the crust of humility all their life." The rhythm and meter in Amanda's speeches are often that of iambic pentameter: "Laura, come here and make a wish on the moon! . . . / A little silver slipper of a moon" (sc. 5).

Although annoying at the time, Amanda's excesses can be viewed in retrospect by Tom with gentle humor—her self-dramatizing in scene 2 with Laura over her leaving the business college, her coquettish manner with Jim, and her two phone conversations. Amanda is at her best (and worst) in the telephone calls to Daughters of the American Revolution (DAR) friends to promote magazine subscriptions that might bring in extra money "to feather the nest and plume the bird," as Tom says. But in scene 3, beneath her gushing descriptions of the serial fiction—"a book that critics already compare to *Gone with the Wind*"—one senses a note of desperation.

Only desperation could prompt Amanda's belief that fragile, withdrawn Laura could marry to find security in life. Aware of Tom's letter from the merchant marine, Amanda warns him in scene 4 that, until Laura is "married, a home of her own, independent. . . . you've got to look out for your sister. . . . because she's young and dependent."

Based on Williams's own sister Rose, whose disability was mental rather than physical, Laura is a delicately drawn, haunting figure. Her defect has caused Laura to withdraw into her own world, lovingly tending her glass collection and playing her father's old phonograph records. Just as Amanda's arias recall her past, so the old songs like "Dardanella" and "Whispering" conjure up the absent father. In his introduction to "The Characters" Williams says of Laura that her "separation increases till she is like a piece of her own glass collection, too exquisitely fragile to move from the shelf."

In its beauty and luminous fragility the glass menagerie symbolizes Laura. She describes it to Jim in scene 7: "Little articles . . . ornaments mostly! Most of them are little animals made out of glass, the tiniest little animals in the world. Mother calls them a glass menagerie!" They are her escape mechanism, as the movies are Tom's and the past is Amanda's.

Despite the signs of Laura's increasing separation from reality, Amanda persists, as if forcing her daughter into activities that are "normal" will make her so. Amanda regards as a betrayal, not a warning signal, Laura's flight from business school, where she was sent to learn skills to obtain a job that would support her. So that Amanda would believe she was in school, Laura has spent nine hours a day wandering in cold parks and visiting the zoo rather than attending the school, where the typing speed test made her hands shake so, her fingers couldn't hit the right keys. In scene 2, when Amanda challenges her about this "deception," Laura can only reply, "It was the lesser of two evils."

Amanda's next attempt is even more unrealistic than her first—to invite to dinner a young man who would, like Amanda's gentleman callers, propose marriage. When in scene 2 Amanda suggests marriage as an alternative to a business career, Laura protests "*(in a tone of frightened apology):* I'm—crippled!" Amanda, undaunted, insists: "Why, you're not crippled, you just have a little defect—hardly noticeable, even! When people have some slight disadvantage like that, they cultivate other things to make up for it—develop charm—and vivacity—and—*charm*! That's all you have to do!"

As he informs his mother in scene 5 that a gentleman caller is indeed coming to dinner, Tom tries to warn her that she "mustn't expect too much of Laura," who might "seem a little peculiar to people outside the house": "She lives in a world of her own—a world of little glass ornaments, Mother." In the play Laura's lameness is seen as the cause of her withdrawal from the world, but it is also a symbol of a more serious, mental condition such as that suffered by Williams's sister Rose. He writes of this with great tenderness in three prose accounts, his autobiography, *Memoirs,* and two short stories, "Portrait of a Girl in Glass" and "The Resemblance between a Violin Case and a Coffin."

In "Portrait," a short version of the dinner event in the play, Williams says of Laura, "She made no positive motion toward the world but stood at the edge of the water, so to speak, with feet that anticipated too much cold to move." He later uses a flower metaphor to describe her state of mind: "I think the petals of her mind had simply closed through fear." The story ends like the play, with the narrator, having deserted his mother and sister, still gripped by guilt when he recalls his sister: "once in a while. . . . a door comes softly and irresistibly open. I hear the tired old music my unknown father left in the place he abandoned as faithlessly as I. I see the faint and sorrowful radiance of the glass, hundreds of little transparent pieces of it in very delicate colors. I hold my breath, for if my sister's face appears among them—the night is hers!"[6]

The fear that characterizes the sister in both short stories is also a manifestation of Laura's personality disorder. With great artistry Williams dramatizes the progression of Laura's initial shyness and withdrawal to her fright when she learns that the visitor is the same Jim O'Connor she had idolized in high school, to her "Terror"—the "legend" seen on the screen as Amanda insists that Laura appear at the table. When she does so, "She is obviously quite faint, her lips trembling, her eyes wide and staring. She moves unsteadily toward the table" (sc. 6).

Williams's dramatic skills are evident both in the characterization of Jim and in the delineation of the action between him and Laura. As the short, magical sequence begins to unfold in scene 7, it is implied that the "long delayed but always expected something we live for" might just be possible for Laura. Jim is now a "high school hero" only to Laura; after graduation "his speed had definitely slowed"; he is now a warehouse clerk along with Tom. Ironically, despite Jim's lack of advancement, he epitomizes the American Dream. He is studying science and public speaking, getting "in on the ground floor. . . . Full steam—*Knowledge*—Zzzzp! *Money*—Zzzzzp!—*Power!* That's the cycle democracy is built on!" He even compares himself to Superman. But at the same time he is a true "gentleman" caller, gentle and understanding. As Laura and Jim, alone in the candlelight, chew gum, talk, and finally dance, Jim draws Laura out of her shell to speak about her glass collection and even to trust him holding the unicorn.

He kisses her gently and then realizes his mistake. But Laura is transformed: "She looks up, smiling. . . . Her look grows brighter even." Then Jim explains about his fiancée Betty. Laura "struggles visibly with her storm. . . . There is a look of almost infinite desolation." Williams conveys the desolation that such a shock would wreak upon a fragile mind by giving Laura only three more words of dialogue in the final scene; she places the unicorn in his hand as "A—souvenir . . ." (Williams's ellipsis) and utters "Yes," when Amanda wishes the hastily departing Jim good luck. Laura's reversion to an even greater withdrawal is indicated by her posture, visibly shrinking from the hurtful reality toward which she will never again venture. She "crouches beside the Victrola to wind it," as Amanda comments: "Things have a way of turning out so badly. I don't believe that I would play the Victrola." Amanda and Tom have their final argument, and he leaves for good.

THE GLASS MENAGERIE

As he recalls his mother and sister in his final speech,
continuing the mood of nostalgia established at the opening, and the "sorrow" of the musical refrain called "Laura's
music," Tom's sense of loss is all the greater. It is not only
his loss of "yesteryear" (the first "legend" to appear on the
backlighted screen) but Laura's loss, to which he responded with desertion, followed by everlasting guilt.

Throughout the drama Tom plays a double role. He is
the son in the action as well as the narrator who looks back
on the events of the past from the perspective of the present.
As narrator, he introduces, explains, interprets, and comments ironically on the action: "The idea of getting a
gentleman caller for Laura. . . . became an obsession," he
says at the beginning of scene 3. "Like some archetype of
the universal unconscious, the image of the gentleman
caller haunted our small apartment."

As "the play is memory," and memory is selective,
Tom's recollections of his mother center on their conflicts.
In the opening scene she is nagging him about his table
manners, and in the course of the play their quarrels mount
in intensity until he leaves the family. Amanda has no
sympathy with his "creative labor," interrupting his writing, challenging his moviegoing in scene 3: "What right
have you got to jeopardize your job?" To her charge that he
is selfish Tom replies: "You think I'm in love with the
Continental Shoemakers? . . . Look! I'd rather somebody

picked up a crowbar and battered out my brains—than go back mornings! I *go!* Every time you come in yelling that Goddamn *'Rise and Shine!' 'Rise and Shine!'* I say to myself, 'How *lucky dead* people are!' But I get up.... I give up all that I dream of doing and being *ever!"* Tom's frustration is justified, but so are Amanda's fears that he will desert them, as his father did.

Williams has an unerring instinct for memorable endings that are not only inevitable but also high drama. As Tom delivers his curtain speech, Amanda and Laura are seen through a scrim in a tableau image that refuses to leave his mind. His guilt at his desertion of them, as he travels through the world, pursues him like Orestes' Furies:

The cities swept about me like dead leaves,
leaves that were brightly colored but torn away
    from the branches.
I would have stopped, but I was pursued by some
                                thing. . . .
Perhaps it was a familiar bit of music.
Perhaps it was only a piece of transparent glass. . . .
I pass the lighted window of a shop where perfume
                                is sold.
The window is filled with pieces of colored glass,
tiny transparent bottles in delicate colors,
    like bits of a shattered rainbow.
Then all at once my sister touches my shoulder.

Although the final scene never fails in its impact, no matter how large or small the theater, some who look only at the text or who are more accustomed to realism than to lyricism would prefer a different ending. Benjamin Nelson feels Williams "has substituted a painfully pretentious narration for what could have been an intense and luminous moment between the two women."[7] Because Nancy Tischler finds the prose "ponderous," it has here been set as blank verse to demonstrate its rhythm and delicacy. She also finds the stage directions, which are so revealing of character, "excessively arty."[8]

While the glass collection is the most recurrent image of Laura, other symbols are the unicorn, blue roses, and candles. All three, like Laura, have no place in this world, being (successively) extinct, nonexistent, and anachronistic. Tom's final line is: "For nowadays the world is lit by lightning! Blow out your candles, Laura—and so goodbye. . . ." (Williams's ellipsis) as, behind the scrim, Laura blows the candles out, ending the play.

The family tragedy is set against the larger social context of the country in the 1930s, when "the huge middle class of America was matriculating in a school for the blind," as Tom reports in his opening speech. There was revolution in Spain and, for the first time, aerial destruction of whole towns, like Guernica, while here, "there was only shouting and confusion . . . disturbances of labor, sometimes pretty violent, in otherwise peaceful cities." In scene

5 the tune "All the World is Waiting for the Sunrise!" drifts in from the Paradise Dance Hall, where, Tom notes, couples dance under "a large glass sphere," with "delicate rainbow colors," while "all the world was waiting for bombardments!" (Williams always chooses popular tunes that are both apt and symbolic.) As the destruction of World War II looms, escape-seeking society might be regarded as a macrocosm of the Wingfield family, where the women seek refuge in old traditions and old tunes, and Tom deserts them to wander the world, only to learn there is no escape.

Williams realized that for the kind of lyric, nonrealistic, plastic theater he was creating, the effect must be total, an integral whole combining the spoken word, characters, movement, visual effects, and sound. Calling for this in play after play, in long and exacting stage directions that are poetic in themselves, he insists that the effects he seeks are "not realistic." But the aura of realism Williams creates, by rooting his poetic plays in concrete imagery and allusion—like songs, brand names such as Celotex and Life Saver, proper names, and amounts of money—misled such critics as Eric Bentley, who insisted that the plays' "realism" was Williams's only virtue.[9]

Williams's "Production Notes," which preface the reading version of *The Glass Menagerie,* call for an "unusual freedom of convention" in presentation: "Expressionism," through "unconventional techniques," argues Williams, achieves "a closer approach to truth. . . . a more penetrating and vivid expression of things as they are." He states that "a new, plastic theater . . . must take the place of the exhausted theater of realistic conventions if the theater is to resume vitality as part of our culture." Noting that the "straight realistic play with . . . its characters who speak exactly as its audience speaks . . . has the same virtue of a photographic likeness," he reminds us of "the unimportance of the photographic in art." He asserts that "truth, life, or reality is an organic thing which the poetic imagination can represent or suggest, in essence, only through transformation, through changing into other forms than those which were merely present in appearance."

Expressionism, the reaction against photographic realism in art, cinema, and theater, assumed importance in the 1920s and 1930s in Europe, with such films as *The Cabinet of Dr. Caligari,* and in America, with plays like O'Neill's *The Great God Brown* and Treadwell's *Machinal.* Reality was transformed, and symbols were used to depict inner thoughts and emotions.

Ironically, Williams's plea for poetic imagination and transcendence of realism to represent "truth, life, or reality" generally went unheeded in the production of his plays during his lifetime. His stage directions were frequently ignored by directors in favor of dependable realism, especially with financial investment at stake. So, the original production of *The Glass Menagerie* discarded the "screen device" Williams calls for to depict the inner lives of the characters, which he also reveals through symbols, setting, and stage effects, as well as action and dialogue.

The "Production Notes" in the reading version of *The Glass Menagerie* include his original directions for a screen device to "give accent to certain values" in the play and provide structure for what "may seem fragmentary rather than architectural." On this screen, or scrim, which, when not backlighted, serves as an interior wall, are to be projected from behind "magic-lantern slides bearing images or titles," explains Williams. (The titles he also calls "legends.") In addition to providing structure and strengthening values, the screen device, Williams believes, would also contribute to the play's "emotional appeal," the "nostalgia, which is the first condition of the play."

Almost all of the visual "images" to be seen on the screen are heightened, romantic pictures of the past, while the titles, or legends, are words that echo the reality of the present. Images include Amanda as a girl on the porch, greeting callers; blue roses; a young man at the door with flowers; Jim as a high school hero; a glamorous magazine cover; a Jolly Roger sailing vessel (the romantic symbol of a drab merchant marine ship). A few images are expressionistic: a "swarm of typewriters" evokes Laura's nightmarish experience at business school, while the "winter scene in a park" reflects her loneliness. Jim as "The Clerk" is in contrast to his picture as "The high school hero." Though not projected on the screen, the grinning photo of the father of the family may be included in the images; it even plays a part when it lights up in scene 4 as if in answer to Tom's lament, "Who in hell ever got himself out of" a "nailed-up coffin?"

The final tableau of Amanda and Laura completes Tom's "memory play" and uses the same scrim on which the images have been projected, now illuminating a living picture, the most vivid of all the images, depicting Tom's "immutable and inexpressible sorrow."

The images from the past evoke memory, which, says Williams, is "nonrealistic" and which may exaggerate "according to the emotional value of the articles it touches." When Williams refers to "magic-lantern slides bearing images or titles" to explain the screen device, he is alluding to a favorite pastime of children when he was growing up. Glass slides about three inches square on which colored pictures illustrating scenes from a story were projected onto a screen by a "magic lantern." Some eight to twelve slides, sometimes accompanied by a brief legend of description or dialogue, told original or familiar stories, like Ali Baba or the fox and the crow. Proust, whom Williams greatly admired, goes into great detail about the pictures his magic lantern projected when he was a child.

While the images Williams calls for primarily relate to the past, the legends are drawn from the present. They may have been suggested by silent movies, in which printed "titles" supplied necessary dialogue or exposition when not conveyed by the actions and lip movements of the actors. Williams's legends express key words and phrases of the spoken dialogue, emphasize Laura's emotions ("Terror!"), or, on a few occasions, comment monosyllabically on the action: "Ah!" (sc. 6); "Ha!" (sc. 7). Sometimes they antici- pate the action to come, as in "The accent of a coming foot" and "The Opening of a Door!" preceding these actions in scene 6.

Image and legend are combined in the image of blue roses, a phrase that recurs in the dialogue. It was Jim's friendly nickname for Laura when they were in high school, coined from her explanation for her absence: "pleurosis." She confides this to Amanda before it is known that the expected gentleman caller and Jim are one and the same. Jim and Laura share the recollection when they are alone together in scene 7. Trying to bolster her confidence, Jim says, "being different is nothing to be ashamed of.... You're one times one!... you—well, you're—*Blue Roses! (Image on screen: Blue Roses.)*" It is the most poignant of all the images, symbolizing Laura's beauty, fragility, and difference, as she replies, "But blue is wrong for—roses."

The screen device was omitted from the original pro- duction of *The Glass Menagerie* probably because director Eddie Dowling, who also played Tom, was unable to reproduce onstage what was called for in the script. But Williams's own sure sense of theater dictated that the screen device be included in the reading version published in 1945.

Fortunately, as Williams's artistry became more and more appreciated, many directors have restored the screen device. The screen symbolizes memory—just as the mind might summon up from the past a phrase or a visual image that serves as the key to recollection, much like Proust's petite madeleine cake. Director Geoffrey Borny relates the importance of the screen device in his production: "It is by means of these nonrealistic staging devices," he says, "that the realistic story is made symbolically significant." [10]

Whether or not the screen device and its images and legends are present, *The Glass Menagerie* has a tremendous emotional impact upon its audiences. The device is only one example of Williams's ability to infuse with poetry and universality such familiar materials as family ties and rifts, old songs and photographs, living and dining rooms with portieres between them, special events celebrated with meals, resurrected clothing, movies, dancing, and hobby collections, like tiny glass animals.

When the acting version of the play was published in 1948 by Dramatists Play Service for use by regional productions, it also omitted the screen device, as it was based on the Broadway production. Although revised, it not only omits the screen device but also contains over a thousand changes in the original script as written by Williams. Most of these were made by the actors and some of them by drama critic George Jean Nathan. The publisher's "Practical Suggestions" confess that "the present edition differs from the book of the play," claiming that the dialogue "to some extent" has been revised by the author. But, to a larger extent, the acting version records the actors again and again taking a facile approach and coarsening the original script by substituting what was easier for them to say, replacing the more poetic Williams dialogue with their conversational "insertions" and "ad libbing," as Williams complains in a letter to Donald Windham.[11]

While Rosamond Gilder was the most perceptive critic in recognizing the value and importance of *The Glass Menagerie,* the other reviewers tempered their enthusiasm, unable to distinguish between the text and the production. Joseph Wood Krutch, who conceded that the play had "a hard substantial core of shrewd observation and deft, economical characterization," nevertheless felt that "this hard core is enveloped in a fuzzy haze of pretentious, sentimental, pseudo-poetic verbiage."[12] Stark Young, who was not only an excellent drama critic but also a Southerner like Williams, criticized the production's "artificial" theatricality but praised the dialogue, especially "the Southern speech in the mother's part."[13]

In the 1987 film version Joanne Woodward is impressive as an Amanda who is energetic and scatterbrained yet sensitive and heroic as well. She evokes the poetry and the rhythm of the lines and captures what Williams termed the natural eloquence of Southern speech. John Malkovich, as Tom, seems to intentionally insert pauses and misplace Williams's textual accents to rob the speeches of any vestige of rhythm and lyricism. Based on a regional stage production using the Dramatists Play Service text, the film is directed by Paul Newman. A good television version (1973) stars Katharine Hepburn (who seems too old for a mother of children in their early twenties) with an excellent supporting cast, including Sam Waterston as Tom, Joanna Miles as Laura, and Michael Moriarty as the gentleman caller.

Notes

1. Rosamond Gilder, *Theatre Arts* 29 (June 1945): 325.

2. Thomas E. Porter, "The Passing of the Old South," *Myth and Modern American Drama* (Detroit: Wayne State University Press, 1969), 158.

3. Delma E. Presley, *The Glass Menagerie: An American Memory* (Boston: G. K. Hall, 1990), 34, 38.

4. Dotson Rader, "Tennessee Williams," *Paris Review* (Fall 1981); reprinted in *Conversations with Tennessee Williams,* ed. Albert J. Devlin (Jackson: University Press of Mississippi, 1986), 334.

5. Stark Young, "The Glass Menagerie," *New Republic* 112, 16 April 1945, 505.

6. *Tennessee Williams: Collected Stories* (New York: New Directions, 1985; London: Secker and Warburg, 1985), 110, 112, 119.

7. Benjamin Nelson, *Tennessee Williams: The Man and His Work* (New York: Ivan Obolensky, 1961), 109.

8. Nancy M. Tischler, "The Distorted Mirror: Tennessee Williams's Self-Portraits," *Mississippi Quarterly* 25 (Fall 1972): 396.

9. Eric Bentley,"Camino Real," *New Republic* 128, 30 March 1953, 30–31.

10. Geoffrey Borny, "The Two *Glass Menageries:* Reading Edition and Acting Edition," in *The Glass Menagerie: Modern Critical Interpretations,* ed. Harold Bloom (New York: Chelsea House, 1988), 107–8, 114.

11. Tennessee Williams, *Letters to Donald Windham, 1940–1965* (New York: Holt, Rinehart and Winston, 1976), 155.

12. Joseph Wood Krutch, "Drama," *Nation* 160, 14 April l945, 424.

13. Young, "Glass Menagerie," 505.

CHAPTER THREE

A Streetcar Named Desire

The dramatic tensions of *A Streetcar Named Desire* are built on contrasts—in theme, in setting, in characters, in language, in action. The structure of the play is that of the journey or quest. A strong visual contrast is established in the opening moments, when a large frame house with "quaintly ornamented gables" is seen. Once it would have been a fine structure, traditionally painted white; now it is "weathered grey, with rickety outside stairs and galleries." Like all Williams's settings, the house is symbolic—a visual image of the decline of the South and of Blanche herself, whose first name means "white" and whose married name is "Grey." The street and its people, their "voices" and the "Blue Piano" of the nearby bar, will serve as backdrop to the action.

As soon as Blanche enters, it can be seen that her appearance is "incongruous" in this neighborhood, whose inhabitants include the two men preceding her, Stanley and Mitch, in work clothes, on their way to bowling. Stanley's voice is the first that is heard distinctly, "(*bellowing*) 'Hey, there! Stella, Baby!'" as he throws at her "a red-stained package from a butcher's." Blanche carries a valise, is "daintily dressed," wearing gloves and a hat, with "something about her uncertain manner, as well as her white clothes, that suggests a moth."

On one level Blanche's opening words ask directions of the women on the stoop; on another they symbolize her life journey and state a major theme of the play: "They told me to take a street-car named Desire, and then transfer to one called Cemeteries and ride six blocks and get off at—Elysian Fields!" "That's where you are now," says Eunice. The Elysian Fields, Virgil's beauteous afterworld inhabited by the blessed dead, are a far cry from the New Orleans locale to which the streetcars have brought Blanche. But the names of the streetcars and their destination symbolize a universal odyssey, as well as Blanche's in particular. As in seven of the nine major plays, the action of *Streetcar* centers upon a visit. The play opens with Blanche's arrival and ends with her departure.

As a girl, Blanche had been "tender and trusting," until her first love at sixteen, a "blinding light" suddenly extinguished by tragedy. Next were "intimacies with strangers," as Blanche sought protection through lovemaking: "People don't see you—*men* don't—don't even admit your existence unless they are making love to you. And you've got to have your existence admitted by someone, if you're going to have someone's protection," she explains to Stella in scene 5. Blanche's quest for security almost attains its goal through marriage to Mitch—but the streetcar trip has an unexpected final destination.

As Eunice lets Blanche into the two rooms in which Stanley and Stella live ("She's got the downstairs here and I got the up"), the interior of the frame house becomes visible. Here the main action will take place; the outside stairs are at stage right. Williams handles the initial exposition with his characteristic skill—in three remarks, as Eunice makes small talk, it is revealed that Blanche is a teacher and that her home is a plantation, "a great big place with white columns," says Eunice, describing a picture she has seen of Belle Reve (Beautiful Dream) and adding, "A place like that must be awful hard to keep up." Underlying the humor of her observation is the truth that will come out shortly. Throughout the play this traditional symbol of the Old South, the plantation Belle Reve, will be contrasted with the harsh reality of the Kowalski dwelling.

Blanche, with near hysteria, reveals to Stella the purpose of her visit: "I was so exhausted by all I'd been through my—nerves broke. . . . I was on the verge of—lunacy, almost! So . . . the high school superintendent—he suggested I take a leave of absence." After breaking the news that Belle Reve has been lost, Blanche launches into the first of her arias, a long, emotional speech about the deaths in the family, "the long parade to the graveyard," the sickness and the struggle of the dying, the horror of disease. "How in hell do you think all that sickness and dying was paid for? Death is expensive, Miss Stella! . . . Sit there and stare at me, thinking I let the place go! . . . Where were *you*! In bed with your—Polack!"

Death, symbolized by the streetcar Cemeteries, Blanche has responded to with Desire, the name of the other streetcar, which brings her to Stella's and to the Elysian Fields of her future. To explain Blanche's character and actions in the present Williams dramatically unfolds her past throughout the play. It is not until scene 9 that Blanche, confronted by Mitch with the "truth" Stanley has told him about her promiscuity, justifies her past behavior: "Death—I used to sit here and she used to sit over there and death was as close as you are. . . . The opposite is desire. . . . Not far from Belle Reve . . . was a camp where they trained young soldiers. On Saturday nights they would go into town to get drunk. . . . and on the way back they would stagger onto my lawn and call—'Blanche! Blanche!'—. . . . Sometimes I slipped outside to answer their calls."

It is also to Mitch, in scene 6, just before he proposes, that Blanche reveals the story of her marriage as a very young girl to Allan Grey: "There was something different about the boy, a nervousness, a softness and tenderness which wasn't like a man's . . . that thing was there. . . . [Williams's ellipsis] He came to me for help. I didn't know that. . . . all I knew was I'd failed him in some mysterious way and wasn't able to give the help he needed but couldn't speak of!" When she comes unexpectedly into a room and discovers him with "an older man who had been his friend for years" (probably in a homosexual encounter, although she doesn't state this), they pretend "that nothing had been discovered." They drive to the Moon Lake Casino, get drunk, dance to the Varsouviana (a polka tune that will reappear in the final scenes), and in the middle of the dance, "unable to stop myself,—I'd suddenly said—'I saw! I know! You disgust me.'" Allan breaks away from her, a shot is heard, they run to the edge of the lake: "He'd stuck the revolver into his mouth and fired—so that the back of his head had been—blown away!"

Her failure to help Allan sexually and her guilt because of his death also explain her promiscuity, as if she were trying to succeed with strangers where she had failed with him. Thomas P. Adler interprets her behavior with the soldiers as a "kind of desperate flailing about for gratification as a compensation for powerlessness." [1] Seeking protection because of her powerlessness, she explains to Stella in scene 5, "I was never hard or self-sufficient enough. When people are soft—soft people have got to court the favor of hard ones. . . . to be seductive—put on soft colors . . . and glow—make a little—temporary magic just in order to pay for—one night's shelter! . . . I've run for protection, Stella, from under one leaky roof to another . . . —because it was storm—all storm, and I was—caught in the center."

She tells Mitch in scene 9: "After the death of Allan— intimacies with strangers was all I seemed able to fill my empty heart with . . . I think it was panic, just panic, that drove me from one to another, hunting for some protection—here and there, in the most—unlikely places" (Williams's ellipsis).

The fact that the soldiers were "young" suggests that Blanche's sexual relations with them is an attempt to compensate for her failure with Allan, whom she always describes as a "boy." Even though she is now in her thirties, this would explain her obsession with such young men, even boys, who would be close to Allan's age when, at sixteen, she fell in love with him. Another possible explanation for Blanche's promiscuity after Allan's death is that, although she is fleeing the past, she is actually reliving it. "If Blanche can satisfy the soldiers' desires . . . perhaps she can remake Allan after the image of a soldier," helping him in fantasy as she failed to do in reality.[2]

On her journey via Desire and Cemeteries toward the Elysian Fields, where in myth the inhabitants drink of the river Lethe to forget their past lives, Blanche's disintegration is carefully detailed by Williams. Her drinking when alone just before Stella enters, her need for liquor when they meet ("I am going to take just one little tiny nip more"), her confession ("—as you must have noticed—I'm—*not* very *well*"), all are prologue to Blanche's initial encounter with Stanley. Although they do not meet until the very end of the opening scene, Williams at the rise of the curtain has visually established the contrast in appearance and demeanor of the two. He develops it further in their first conversation, during which Stanley indicates she wasn't expected, takes off his shirt, and says, "I'm afraid I'll strike you as being the unrefined type." Their verbal sparring, with underlying sexual innuendo, will intensify in the next scene.

The violence of the poker night in scene 3 produces fear and flight in Blanche, who, after Stella and Stanley have reunited, descends the steps "fearfully" and "looks right and left as if for a sanctuary." At that point Mitch enters, a hope of sanctuary for Blanche. Her fantasy refuge is Shep Huntleigh, a wealthy Texan and former college beau, whom she mentions to Stella in scene 4. Blanche believes they should both escape: "Your fix is worse than mine is!... I'm going to *do* something.... But you've given in. And that isn't right, you're not old! You can get out." Stella answers, "I'm not in anything I want to get out of."

Overheard by Stanley is Blanche's aria, which follows, about his "ape-like" bestiality: "Night falls and the other apes gather! There in the front of the cave, all grunting like him, and swilling and gnawing and hulking! His poker night!—you call it—this party of apes!" She concludes, "In this dark march toward whatever it is we're approaching. . . . *Don't—don't hang back with the brutes!*" (Williams's ellipsis).

Fearful of losing Stella to an adversary beyond his comprehension, Stanley is swift in his revenge. That he is investigating Blanche's past comes out casually in scene 5: "Say, do you happen to know somebody named Shaw?" Blanche's voice has a note of "fear" and she seems "faint," her expression one of "almost panic," as she questions Stella when they are alone about whether she has heard any "unkind gossip." Blanche's hysteria mounts as her hand shakes holding a glass of coke, and she screams when it spills over. She confides to Stella that she has been pretending to be "prim and proper" with Mitch: "I want to *deceive* him enough to make him—want me." Stella asks, "Do you want *him*?" "I want to *rest*!" says Blanche. "I want to breathe quietly again! Yes—I *want* Mitch . . . *very badly*! Just think! If it happens! I can leave here and not be anyone's problem." At the beginning of scene 6 Williams describes Blanche's personality as "neurasthenic."

Her hope of refuge with Mitch seems to be fulfilled by the end of that scene, as playing the prim and proper lady leads to his proposal. But Stanley's revenge begins with the revelations to Stella of what he has mentioned earlier: "I've got th' dope on your big sister. . . . That girl calls *me* common!" Stella may be surprised, but the audience is not—Williams has been careful to reveal hints all along about Blanche's past, from Stanley's casual inquiry about the Flamingo Hotel in Laurel, to her confession to Stella that she hasn't been "so good the last two years," to the encounter with the Young Collector at the end of scene 5. Blanche flirts with, kisses, and then dismisses him with the words "I've got to be good—and keep my hands off children."

In the final three scenes Williams uses the Varsouviana polka tune heard earlier as sweet and stately, now blended with jungle sounds and shadows, to emphasize Blanche's disintegration. It becomes a "rapid, feverish polka tune" at the opening of scene 9, as Williams tells us: "The music is in her mind; she is drinking to escape it and the sense of disaster closing in on her." Here he uses sound effects to suggest his character's mind, just as he used the images and legends in *The Glass Menagerie* to depict the interior lives of Amanda, Tom, and Laura.

In scene 9 Mitch's tearing the paper lantern from the light bulb is symbolic of the dramatic action itself. This single cruel gesture exposes Blanche's age, which she has tried to cover up, just as Stanley has exposed her past, belied by her prim and proper behavior. It also evokes her defense: "I don't want realism. . . . I'll tell you what I want. Magic! . . . I try to give that to people. I misrepresent things to them. I don't tell truth, I tell what *ought* to be truth." As noted, she defends her sexual behavior as her response to the death that surrounded her at Belle Reve: "Death. . . . The opposite is desire. So do you wonder? How could you posssibly wonder!"

The final degradation for a woman of Blanche's sensibility occurs when she asks Mitch to marry her and he rejects her: "You're not clean enough to bring in the house with my mother." She ends the scene screaming; "her throat is tightening with hysteria," as Mitch fumbles to attempt a sexual union: "Fire! Fire! Fire!" She will not escape from Stanley, however.

Stanley's closing line in the penultimate scene is shocking, but it is not unexpected if one recalls Williams's initial description of Stanley when he enters the house to encounter Blanche for the first time. Stanley's every line and action in the play develop this descriptive passage in scene 1:

Animal joy in his being is implicit in all his movements and attitudes. Since earliest manhood the center of his life has been pleasure with women, the giving and taking of it, not with weak indulgence, dependently, but with the power and pride of a richly feathered male bird among hens. Branching out from this complete and satisfying center are all the auxiliary channels of his life . . . everything that is his, that bears his emblem of the gaudy seed-bearer. He sizes women up at a glance, with sexual classifications, crude images flashing into his mind and determining the way he smiles at them.

He speaks the play's opening lines: "Hey, there! Stella, Baby! . . . Catch!" and throws the meat to her. The sexual innuendo is apparent to the women on the stoop:

> NEGRO WOMAN: What was that package he th'ew at 'er? . . .
> EUNICE: You hush, now!
> NEGRO WOMAN: Catch *what!*"

Blanche, "daintily dressed," appears, as the woman "continues to laugh."

In his first meeting with Blanche at the end of scene 1 they are alone; he offers her a drink.

BLANCHE: No, I—rarely touch it.

STANLEY: Some people rarely touch it, but it touches them often. . . . How long you here for, Blanche?

BLANCHE: I—don't know yet.

STANLEY: You going to shack up here?

Shack up is army slang that would come naturally to an ex-GI like Stanley, who is proud of having been in the Two-forty-first Engineers. It was usually a question asked of native women by GIs looking for a brief sexual encounter. That Blanche seems to understand might be puzzling at this time, but it anticipates her asking Mitch in scene 6, when he admits he knows no French, "Voulez-vous couchez avec moi ce soir?" The question was another familiar approach of GIs to women abroad. Thus, in scene 9 her tale of slipping out to meet young soldiers from the nearby army camp comes as no surprise. Stanley's revelation of Blanche's past to Stella includes his comment on the "army camp near Laurel and your sister's was one of the places called 'Out-of-Bounds.'"

In her encounter with Stanley in scene 2, when he is demanding an explanation for the loss of Belle Reve, Blanche, knowing Stanley has "unpacked" her trunk, attempts to gain an advantage by flirting with him. Having drawn the curtains between the two rooms (kitchen and bedroom) which make up the apartment, Blanche puts on her dress and asks Stanley to button up the back. She opens the drapes: "You may enter!"

> STANLEY: I can't do nothing with them.
> BLANCHE: You men with your big clumsy fingers. May I have a drag on your cig?

The last expression, and Blanche will use more like these, was a well-known "opener" with which women seeking further acquaintance approached soldiers.

> Blanche: Would you think it possible that I was once considered to be—attractive?
> Stanley: Your looks are okay.

In reply to Stanley's "there is such a thing in this State of Louisiana as the Napoleonic code, according to which whatever belongs to the wife belongs to the husband also—and vice versa," Blanche exclaims, "My, but you have an impressive judicial air! (*She sprays herself with her atomizer; then playfully sprays him with it. He seizes the atomizer and slams it down on the dresser. She throws back her head and laughs.*)"

> STANLEY: If I didn't know that you was my wife's sister I'd get ideas about you!
> BLANCHE: Such as what!
> STANLEY: Don't play so dumb. You know what!

A STREETCAR NAMED DESIRE

It is important to realize that Blanche in this scene is relying upon the only weapon she has, her sexuality, to save her from being held responsible for the loss of Belle Reve. The provocativeness, the flattering of the male, the invitation to physical contact by way of the buttons, are all geared to having Stanley accept her explanation that the plantation was lost through debt, that she is not "cheating" them out of a share of sale money. With Stella afterward Blanche is honest: "We thrashed it out. I feel a bit shaky, but I think I handled it nicely. . . . called him a little boy and laughed—and flirted! Yes—I was flirting with your husband, Stella!"

She will also use her sexuality to gain Mitch's attention in scene 3 during the poker night, once she finds out that he is not married: "She takes off the blouse and stands in her pink silk brassiere and white skirt in the light through the portieres." When Stella calls her attention to this, Blanche moves out of the light, and then, when Stella goes into the bathroom, Blanche "moves back into the streak of light. She raises her arms and stretches, as she moves indolently back to the chair. . . . Mitch rises at the table." Stanley comes into the bedroom, turns off the radio, "stops short at the sight of Blanche in the chair," and returns to the poker table. When Mitch is inattentive during the game and is asked what he is doing, Stanley replies, "He was looking through them drapes," then jumps up, and "jerks roughly at curtains to close them," almost as if he is jealous of Mitch's looking at Blanche.

Blanche's approach to Mitch contrasts with the way she behaves with Stanley, though with both men there is desperation beneath her surface gaiety. W. David Sievers attributes her behavior to "sexual anxiety. . . . [H]er almost hysterical drive is to find protection and security." [3] Geraldine Thorsten's study of women and power in Lillian Hellman's plays of the same period points out that sexuality was one of the few means of gaining power women had at that time. [4] Blanche might have been successful in using her sexuality to gain an advantage over both men, except that Stanley overhears her attacking him to Stella. Rather than lose Stella, he will go to any lengths, just as Blanche has done through desperation. Although Mitch accepts Blanche as prim and proper, Stanley has known from their first meeting that she has "been around." It is his desire for revenge as well as his wish to hold on to Stella which prompts him to investigate Blanche's past, where he finds more than even he suspected.

As Williams was to state in a 1978 interview, "Stanley was pretty primitive and primordial in his instincts, but in many ways defensible. He was reacting with an animal's instinct to protect its own, its own terrain from invasion, by that element that he could not comprehend, which happened to be Blanche." [5]

Loyalty to Mitch requires that he be told about Blanche, as Stanley informs Stella in scene 7: "We were in the same outfit [in the army] together. . . . We work in the same plant and now on the same bowling team. . . . he's not going to jump in a tank with a school of sharks." Then in scene 8 Stanley plays his trump card: he gives Blanche a "birthday remembrance," a bus ticket back to Laurel. Blanche rushes off to her only place of privacy in the house, the bathroom. "The Varsouviana music steals in softly" and will recur with increasing intensity until the play ends. When Stella charges him with cruelty, Stanley defends himself, his marriage, his relationship with Stella, and his revenge: "Wasn't we happy together? Wasn't it all okay? Till she showed here. Hoity-toity, describing me as an ape."

His revenge will be physical as well as emotional. By the beginning of scene 10, her last refuge, Mitch, snatched from her by Stanley, Blanche already has left the real world. Like Amanda, who puts on a "girlish frock" to escape reality, Blanche is dressed in a "crumpled white satin evening gown. . . . placing the rhinestone tiara on her head . . . murmuring excitedly as if to a group of spectral admirers." "Improvising feverishly," she says she will be going away to join Shep Huntleigh, where she will be appreciated, not "casting my pearls before swine!" The insult prompts Stanley's cruel rejoinder, "there wasn't no wire. . . . there isn't no millionaire. . . . I've been on to you from the start! Not once did you pull any wool over this boy's eyes!" Blanche's last move is to attempt to phone and then wire Shep Huntleigh: "In desperate, desperate circumstances! Help me! Caught in a trap." The message describes not only Blanche but such male Williams characters as Chance Wayne and Lawrence Shannon.

"The gaudy seed-bearer" Stanley appears in his red pajamas, awaiting the announcement of the birth of his son. To him Blanche, even in her present state of desperation, is a woman, and to Stanley women mean one thing only— sex. He interprets her hysterical actions as provocation, even her defensively breaking the bottle as "rough house": "Oh! So you want some rough house!" The rape will destroy Blanche's fragile sanity, but Stanley believes, "We've had this date with each other from the beginning!" The dichotomy of the play reaches a climax with "the ravishment of the tender, the sensitive, the delicate, by the savage and brutal forces of modern society," to quote Williams's defense of the scene when the Hollywood censors sought to eliminate it in the film version.[6] On Broadway an audible shock wave swept through the first audiences at this point of the play, so well-known now, that it is anticipated.

But Williams always carefully prepares his dramas for developments that may be shocking but inevitable. Stanley's cruelty to Blanche has been delineated throughout the play, from the crudeness of his first interview, through the birthday party "gift" of a ticket back to Laurel, to Stella's chastisement in scene 8, "You needn't have been so cruel to someone alone as she is." To which Stanley can only retort, with characteristic sexual innuendo, "Delicate piece she is." Stella's reply reminds us of the enormity of the destruction Stanley is about to wreak: "She is. She was. You didn't know Blanche as a girl. Nobody, nobody, was tender and trusting as she was. But people like you abused her, and forced her to change."

Even Blanche has a premonition of what might occur, but she puts it out of her mind. She tells Mitch in scene 6: "He hates me. Or why would he insult me? Of course there is such a thing as the hostility of—perhaps in some perverse kind of way he—No! To think of it makes me... (*She makes a gesture of revulsion.*)" (Williams's ellipsis).

In contrast to her appearance at the opening of the play and the hope that arrival implies, Blanche's departure for the state mental institution is along the same path in the final scene. Williams's sure sense of theater always develops the action to its one inevitable conclusion. Asked about the ending, Williams observed that Blanche "had personal great strength and personal vulnerability that was finally broken. . . . It was the only solution. . . . She was not adaptable to the circumstances as they were, that the world had imposed on her. . . . she was broken on the rock of the world; I find her a sympathetic character, but I also find Stanley sympathetic."[7] True to his narrow code of self-interest and self-protection, from which he has never departed, Stanley will lie about the rape of Blanche, and Stella, even though she may have her doubts, will believe him because she has to.

All of Williams's dramatic artistry is displayed in the final scene. Earlier motifs are reprised—the disheveled poker-playing group in contrast to Blanche's delicate concern with appearance and the right costume for what she believes to be a trip involving Shep Huntleigh and Stella's conflict between her loyalty to Stanley and the baby and her guilt about committing Blanche. Finally, there is Blanche's response to the doctor, whose single gesture of removing his hat and calling her "Miss DuBois" indicates that he is a gentleman and evokes Blanche's final line: "Whoever you are—I have always depended on the kindness of strangers."

The scrim that serves as the back wall of the apartment lights up to reveal the street outside. As the card game continues and Stanley consoles Stella through the only bond between them ("voluptuously, soothingly. . . . his fingers find the opening of her blouse"), Blanche departs along the same path she entered, "escorted" by the doctor, a nurse carrying the same valise.

Before Elia Kazan had accepted the offer to direct the play, Williams wrote him "to clarify [his] intentions in this play," a letter Kazan reproduces in part in his memoirs: "I remember you asked me what should an audience feel for Blanche. Certainly pity. It is a tragedy with the classic aim of producing a catharsis of pity and terror and in order to do that, Blanche must finally have the understanding and compassion of the audience. This without creating a black-dyed villain in Stanley." [8]

The language, symbolism, and theatrical effects create the extra dimension Williams sought, beyond realism. The heightened language only sounds realistic, for Williams excels in creating dialogue that is unique and individual to its speaker. Stanley's idiom is made up of army and conventional slang, trite expressions ("Haven't fallen in, have you?" as a way of hurrying someone from the bathroom), street grammar, curses, and grunts like "huh?" His sentences are short. But there is humor too, however crude, as well as an unquestioning trust in authority, such as the Napoleonic code. Using all of these marks of character, Williams goes one step beyond: Stanley has a poetry of his own that is particularly his; it is heightened, alliterative, rhythmic. The words are exact—not at all those a "real" Stanley would know or choose, even though they are monosyllabic. He is going through Blanche's trunk in scene 2: "Open your eyes to this stuff! . . . Look at these feathers and furs that she come here to preen herself in! . . . What is these here? Fox pieces! (*He blows on them*). Genuine fox fur-pieces, a half a mile long! Where are your fox-pieces, Stella? Bushy snow-white ones, no less! Where are your white fox pieces?"

Making Blanche an English teacher allows Williams full play for lyricism and literary allusions, which are quite in character. Questioned by Stanley, she describes the furs as "a tribute from an admirer." Her long speeches, verbal arias, develop metaphors while building rhythmically to a climactic sentence. The "ape" speech in scene 4, which Stanley overhears and which sets in motion his cruel revenge, intensifies beyond the "real" in its word choice. At the same time the speech is analogous to the action: "Bearing the raw meat home from the kill in the jungle" is reminiscent of the opening of the play, while "grunting . . . swilling and gnawing and hulking! [recalls] his poker night!" Falling back on trite and proverbial expressions, as she does from time to time ("Forewarned is forearmed"), demonstrates her anxiety and hardly warrants Cohn's charge that her images are "stale," "incongruous," and "pretentious." [9]

Stella in scene 4 defends her life with Stanley: "There are things that happen between a man and a woman in the dark—that sort of make everything else seem—unimportant." Blanche's reply exemplifies Williams's dialogue, which is appropriate to the character, while at the same time, through its choice of concrete imagery, it is lyric and symbolic as well:

> BLANCHE: What you are talking about is brutal desire—just—Desire!—the name of that rattle-trap street-car that bangs through the Quarter, up one old narrow street and down another. . . . [Williams's ellipsis]
> STELLA: Haven't you ever ridden on that street-car?
> BLANCHE: It brought me here.

While the women are speaking of sexual desire, James Hafley notes an additional connotation of the word. As termed by Blanche the "opposite" of death, *desire* may be "a longing for transcendence," he suggests.[10]

The supporting roles of Stella and Mitch are in almost direct opposition to the characters of Blanche and Stanley, despite a close relationship as sibling and friend. Coming from the same background as Blanche, accustomed to an environment of comfort and culture, Stella warns Blanche in the opening scene that Stanley is not like the "men that we went out with at home." He is "a different species. . . . you can't describe someone you're in love with!" She shows Blanche a picture of Stanley in uniform—a master sergeant in the engineers' corps. Like many other women during wartime, Stella would have had the opportunity to meet men other than those on her own social level, for the uniform was a great leveler. By leaving home, Stella avoided the family crises that Blanche had to face: illnesses, deaths, and financial difficulties that resulted in the loss of Belle Reve. Because of Stanley's overwhelming physical attraction, Stella has been able to abandon her previous values and to adjust to life in a situation that is "Elysian Fields" for her. In time the attraction of the "colored lights" might wear off, but at present she is contented and happy with Stanley.

Yet she is not insensitive to Blanche's desperation and more and more comes to take her side against Stanley. She upbraids Stanley for his cruelty to her sister, but in the final scene she cannot help Blanche at the expense of the marriage and the child. She chooses Stanley: "I couldn't believe her story and go on living with Stanley." Eunice advises her: "Don't ever believe it. Life has got to go on." Stella's action in this scene shows her literally running out on Blanche. As Blanche tries to evade the matron, "Stella runs out to the porch" and "rushes into Eunice's embrace on the porch." She knows she has failed her sister in her hour of need: "What have I done to my sister? Oh, God, what have I done to my sister?"

Although Stanley and Mitch were war buddies in the Two-forty-first Engineers, Mitch, as Blanche observes, "seems—superior to the others." His sensitivity Stella attributes to the fact that "his mother is sick." Whether it is his sick mother or the death of the woman he cared for, Mitch comes across as a sensitive person in his first encounter with Blanche during Stanley's poker night. Like Stella, Blanche is prepared to settle for less, so that she plays the prim and proper lady with Mitch, who is quite dazzled by her. As he says in scene 6, "I like you to be exactly the way that you are, because in all my—experience—I have never known anyone like you."

Williams excels in encounter scenes between a man and a woman, and scene 6 is no exception. The level of Mitch's interests in life, besides poker and bowling, is indicated by his conversation about his weight, his jacket—

"very light weight alpaca"—and his membership in the New Orleans Athletic Club, to which Blanche responds with forced animation. Blanche is actually guiding the conversation, as she adroitly moves the subject to herself. She complains of her treatment by Stanley, Mitch mentions his mother's question about Blanche's age when told he liked her, Blanche relates the story of Allan's death, and Mitch proposes: "You need somebody. And I need somebody, too. Could it be—you and me, Blanche?" Their marriage could mean salvation for Blanche, as her reply indicates: "Sometimes—there's God—so quickly!"

Sadly, the next time Mitch appears, in scene nine, he has been told of Blanche's past and is interested only in "what [he has] been missing all summer": "I don't think I want to marry you any more. . . . You're not clean enough to bring in the house with my mother." Yet in the final scene he, like Stella, suffers remorse for Blanche's fate, for which he blames Stanley, accusing him and trying to strike him: "I'll kill you!" Steve holds him back, and Mitch "collapses at the table, sobbing."

In his foreword to *Camino Real* Williams states that "a symbol in a play has only one legitimate purpose, which is to say a thing more directly and simply and beautifully than it could be said in words." In *Streetcar* verbal, visual, and technical (sound and light) symbolism combine to achieve "poetic drama," to use Williams's term for his plays. Light is one of the most prevalent symbols. Stanley's sole original metaphor is "colored lights" for the sex he and Stella enjoy. Blanche's "light" images are related to Allan, her first and only love: "It was like you suddenly turned a blinding light on something that had always been half in shadow." After he kills himself, "then the searchlight which had been turned on the world was turned off again and never for one moment since has there been any light that's stronger than this—kitchen—candle" (sc. 6). The light of birthday candles, usually associated with celebration, is the central metaphor of Blanche's lament in scene 8: "candles aren't safe . . . candles burn out in little boys' and girls' eyes, or wind blows them out and after that happens, electric light bulbs go on and you see too plainly." Candles also suggest the attraction of the flame for "moth"-like Blanche. As the action builds, the symbol of fire (for passion) is introduced, first in Blanche's cries of "Fire!" in scene 9 and again just before the rape, Stanley's symbol of "colored lights" turns into the "shadows and lurid reflections [which] move sinuously as flames along the wall spaces."

Blanche's constant bathing suggests the traditional association of water with purification; there is also the implication of Lethe and forgetfulness. In her final aria in the last scene, beautifully lyric in its assonance, alliteration, and onomatopoeia, she says she will die on the sea "of eating an unwashed grape" and be "sewn up in a clean white sack and dropped overboard . . . into an ocean as blue as my first lover's eyes!"

Among Williams's unpublished papers is a 1943 melodramatic verse play called *The Spinning Song,* which originally may have been the "Southern epic" suggested to and rejected by MGM, when he worked for them that year. In his introductory note Williams says that the play, "the story of the disintegration of a land-owning Southern family," had its origins in his seeing Eisenstein's film classic *Alexander Nevsky:*

> Its pictorial drama and poetry of atmosphere . . . made me wonder if it were not possible to achieve something analogous to this in a poetic drama for the stage. . . . I determined to think in more plastic or visual terms.To write sparingly but with complete lyricism, and to build the play in a series of dramatic pictures.No play written in such creative terms could be naturalistic. . . . It would have to be a . . . tragedy purified by poetry and music.[11]

In another forerunner of *Streetcar,* an unpublished one-act called *Interior: Panic,* Williams calls for "irregularities of design," including "lurid projections" on "white plaster walls," to symbolize "the hysteria" of the Blanche character.[12]

The Freudian symbolism of *Streetcar,* as well as the dialogue, action, and characterization, anticipates the rape of Blanche. Mitch's gesture of "rooting" for the key in Blanche's handbag in scene 6 is repeated in the climactic scene 10. While in the street outside the Negro Woman picks up the prostitute's handbag and "roots" through it, inside Stanley approaches Blanche. At the beginning of that scene Blanche's smashing of the hand mirror may be influenced by Cocteau's brilliant use of the image of breaking glass of an enclosure to symbolize intercourse in his film *Beauty and the Beast.* (A breaking mirror is used as a substitute for Stanley's famous line in the film version of *Streetcar,* when Williams had to fight the Breen Office censors even to include this symbol and the implication of rape.) When in the same scene Stanley opens a bottle of beer and proffers it as a "loving-cup" to Blanche, "a geyser of foam shoots up." Then, as the blue piano becomes "the roar of an approaching locomotive" (earlier identified with Stanley as unstoppable), he "takes a step toward her, biting his tongue, which protrudes between his lips." His final gesture to Blanche in the last scene is symbolic of the rape itself, as the stage direction indicates: "Seizes the paper lantern, tearing it off the light bulb and extends it toward her. She cries out as if the lantern was herself."

The light bulb and the colored paper lantern covering it represent the contrast between the reality that Blanche cannot face and the magic she wishes to create, as she explains in scene 9: "I don't want realism. . . . I'll tell you what I want. Magic!" In a practical sense as well, for appearance is all-important, she wishes to shield her aging face from the "truth" of bright lights. Observes Mitch: "You never want to go out till after six and then it's always some place that's not lighted much. . . . I've never had a real good look at you, Blanche. . . . Let's turn the light on here."

In the same scene death is symbolized by the blind, dark shawled Mexican Woman, whose single line—"flowers for the dead"—is contrapuntal to Blanche's speech about desire as a response to death when she slipped away from her seat beside a relative's deathbed and answered the calls of the drunken young soldiers: "Later the paddy-wagon would gather them up like daisies . . . the long way home" (Williams's ellipsis).

At the end of the play Stella's baby is brought in by Eunice and placed in Stella's arms just as she calls out after the departing Blanche. It confirms and strengthens the marriage, although it could be surmised that Stella might turn from Stanley to the child. This is the resolution provided in the film, which dictated punishment for Stanley, as Stella at the very end repulses his advances with "Don't touch me; don't ever touch me again," and runs upstairs with the baby in her arms. The film's director, Elia Kazan, reveals in his memoirs that he wrote this line for the film, an ending Williams considered a "contradiction" of his intentions: "They made Stella decide never to sleep with Stanley again, which is a total contradiction to the meaning of the play; he does, the meaning of the play is that he does go on with her." [13]

Strong contrasts in color and sound symbolically reinforce the action. Born under the sign of Virgo, Blanche is dressed in white at her first entrance (changed to powder blue in the original production) and, in her final scene, wears a jacket she describes as "Della Robbia blue. The blue of the robe in the old Madonna pictures." The religious allusion may be only partly ironic. Stanley ("a richly feathered male bird," according to Williams's initial description) wears brightly colored bowling shirts and later red silk pajamas. The poker night Williams relates to van Gogh's billiard parlor in his painting *All Night Cafe,* with bright primary colors (not observed in the original production) for a macho effect of "men at the peak of their physical manhood, as coarse and direct and powerful as the primary colors." Giorgio DeChirico is another artist Williams refers to, in *Summer and Smoke,* to explain a theatrical mood he wishes to create. An exhibition of his paintings in Key West in 1986 revealed Williams as a gifted amateur, with a strong interest in expressionism. There were rose tattoos and lonely figures in looming night streets.

Contrasting sound and visual effects mount in intensity in the final scenes. The stately Varsouviana polka introduced at the end of scene 1, when Allan is first mentioned, and which suggests Blanche's social surroundings at Belle Reve, now distorts in a nightmarish tempo. In contrast, the "Blue Piano" heard at the opening and throughout typifies New Orleans. As the play reaches its climax in scene 10, the effects become more and more expressionistic to reflect Blanche's emotional and mental state. When Stanley advances into the bedroom, "lurid reflections appear on the walls . . . grotesque and menacing." At the same time, foreshadowing Stanley's attack, street violence is revealed through the "back wall of the rooms, which have become transparent." The sound of the Blue Piano grows from barely audible to "louder," and its sound "turns into the roar of an approaching locomotive." Then "inhuman jungle voices rise up," when Stanley, like the unstoppable locomotive, approaches Blanche. As Stanley lifts Blanche and carries her to the bed, "the hot trumpet and drums from the Four Deuces sound loudly."

Just as a composer will use the drumbeat as portent, so Williams directs that in the final scene the "drums sound very softly," as Blanche sees the doctor and matron and slips back into the apartment "with a peculiar smile, her eyes wide and brilliant." As the sound effects here reflect her mental instability, the Varsouviana (which earlier recalled Allan) now, to recall the rape, is "filtered into a weird distortion accompanied by the cries and noises of the jungle," heard in the previous scene. The dialogue, simple phrases like "Now, Blanche," echoes and reverberates, so that the audience hears it as it sounds to Blanche.

A final recurring symbol that might be noted is that of the game, or contest, to reflect the conflict between Blanche and Stanley. An earlier version of the play was titled *The Poker Night,* suggesting that the game of poker is a central metaphor for the larger and more deadly contest between the principals. Johan Huizinga points out that "play . . . is an activity which proceeds within certain limits of time and space, in a visible order, according to rules freely accepted, and outside the sphere of necessity or material utility." [14] The idea of "play" as symbol of a real-life contest is well suited to Williams's conception of the "timeless world" of a drama. Stanley's dictating the rules as captain of the bowling team and host of the poker games foreshadows his winning the conflict with Blanche.

The play opened on Broadway in December 1947, directed by Elia Kazan and starring Jessica Tandy as Blanche and Marlon Brando as Stanley. The direction by Kazan, whose background was the Group Theater and the realistic plays of the 1930s, was strong on realism and short on poetry. Unfortunately for Williams and for the American theater, the play was such a commercial success that no one ever questioned whether Kazan was the best director for Williams until the fiasco with *Camino Real*.

Robert Brustein finds that "Stanley, as *written* by Williams, is a highly complex and ambiguous character, one who can be taken either as hero or as villain. As a social or cultural figure, Stanley is a villain, in mindless opposition to civilization and culture. . . . As a psychological or sexual figure, however, Stanley exists on a somewhat more heroic moral plane. He is akin to those silent, sullen gamekeepers and grooms of D. H. Lawrence . . . whose sexuality, though violent, is unmental, unspiritual, and, therefore, in some way free from taint." He observes that because of "the personal values Brando contributed . . . Stanley . . . emerged as a more appealing, a more sympathetic, and (most important) a more sensitive character than Williams created." Brustein also notes that, when Anthony Quinn took over the role and played Stanley "more like the thick-headed antagonist Williams intended, the focus of the play shifted back to Blanche." [15]

At the time only critic Harold Clurman, himself a director, recognized that Stanley as written (the play was published before it opened) and Stanley as performed by Brando were very different. Clurman pointed out that the "lack of balance and perspective" in Kazan's direction meant that, "for almost more than two-thirds of the play, the audience identifies with Stanley. His 'low jeering' is seconded by the audience's laughter." Clurman observes that some of the first reviewers "thought Blanche DuBois a 'boozy prostitute,' and others believed her a nymphomaniac. Such designations are not only inaccurate but reveal a total failure to understand the author's intention and the theme of the play: . . . that aspiration, sensitivity, departure from the norm are battered, bruised, and disgraced in our world today." [16]

Brando's interpretation also has been responsible for slanting much of the later criticism of the play. Eric Bentley finds that Stanley's "tough talk . . . mask[s] . . . a suffering, sensitive soul." [17] Even by the 1970s' new awareness, Ruby Cohn can defend Stanley's cruelty: "His cruellest gesture in the play is to tear the paper lantern off the light bulb, in order to hand it to Blanche. His other rough acts are understandable. . . . We do not see Stanley hit Stella [who is pregnant, and whom he has struck before, as Eunice points out] and we do not see him rape Blanche; the first deed is mitigated by his contrition, and the second by Blanche's provocation. . . . [H]e is a faithful friend to Mitch and a satisfying husband to Stella." [18]

The secondary roles of Stella and Mitch, played by Kim Hunter and Karl Malden, were well served by these two actors, who also appear in the film version. Although these parts are less "showy," they are all-important, bringing out the very characteristics lacking in Stanley and Blanche, qualities whose absence contributes to the catastrophe. Mitch has the sensitivity to and the respect for women lacking in Stanley, who limits the function of women in his life to the two rooms of the setting—a kitchen and a bedroom. Stella is able to adjust to the reality of life as Blanche never can, even though the adjustment, it must be recognized, is eased by the strong sexual union with Stanley.

The reviews were almost all favorable, and the play won both the Pulitzer and the Critics' Circle awards. Wolcott Gibbs praised it in the *New Yorker* of 13 December 1947 as "a brilliant implacable play about the disintegration of a woman, or if you like, of a society." Mary McCarthy, however, attacked the characterization of

Blanche as "thin, sleezy [*sic*] stuff . . . embellished . . . with all sorts of decorations. . . . She who has never spoken an honest word in her life is allowed, indeed encouraged, to present her life to the audience as a vocational decision, an artist's election of the beautiful, an act of supreme courage, the choice of the thorny way." [19]

A far cry from McCarthy is the appraisal by Frank Rich reviewing the 1992 Broadway revival: "Depending on your feelings about *Long Day's Journey into Night, A Streetcar Named Desire* is either the greatest or second-greatest play ever written by an American." [20]

Although the film version preserves nearly intact the performances of Brando, Hunter, Malden, and some of the minor characters, Hollywood required a star in the leading role. Tandy, who had created a memorable stage Blanche, was then virtually unknown in America. She was replaced by Vivien Leigh, who created only a surface outline of Blanche. Perhaps even more damaging, she "threw away" some of the important lines completely, lines that possibly meant little to her and therefore can mean nothing to the audience.

Since its original production, *Streetcar* has been revived frequently and studied consistently in high schools and colleges throughout the country. Blanche DuBois and Stanley Kowalski have become tags for typing real or fictional characters who are soft and sensitive or macho and animalistic. Blanche's exit line has passed into the catalog of the readily recognizable, appearing in speeches, editorials, and advertisements. In *Memoirs* Williams speaks of Blanche as "a relatively imperishable creature of the stage." He observes that "nearly all of her cries to the world in her season of desperation have survived because they were true cries of her embattled heart; that is what gave them the truth which has made them live on, echoing in the hearts of so many known and unknown ladies."[21]

Notes

1. Thomas P. Adler, *A Streetcar Named Desire: The Moth and the Lantern* (Boston: G. K. Hall, 1990), 43.

2. Donald Pease, "Reflections on Moon Lake: The Presences of the Playwright," in *Tennessee Williams: A Tribute,* ed. Jac Tharpe (Jackson: University Press of Mississippi, 1977), 839.

3. W. David Sievers, "Tennessee Williams and Arthur Miller," *Freud on Broadway: A History of Psychoanalysis and the American Drama* (New York: Cooper Square Publishers, 1955), 378.

4. Geraldine Thorsten, "Women and Power in Lillian Hellman's Major Plays" (Master's thesis, Lehman College, 1990).

5. Cecil Brown, "Interview with Tennessee Williams," *Partisan Review* 45 (1978); reprinted in *Conversations with Tennessee Williams,* ed. Albert J. Devlin (Jackson: University Press of Mississippi, 1986), 266.

6. Thomas H. Pauly, *An American Odyssey: Elia Kazan*

A STREETCAR NAMED DESIRE

and American Culture (Philadelphia: Temple University Press, 1983), 132.

7. Brown, "Interview," 277.

8. Elia Kazan, *A Life* (New York: Alfred A. Knopf, 1988), 330.

9. Ruby Cohn, "The Garrulous Grotesques of Tennessee Williams," *Dialogue in American Drama* (Bloomington: Indiana University Press, 1971), 105.

10. James Hafley, "Abstraction and Order in the Language of Tennessee Williams," in Tharpe, *Tennessee Williams,* 755.

11. MS, September 1943, Humanities Research Center, University of Texas at Austin. Quoted in C. W. E. Bigsby, *A Critical Introduction to Twentieth-Century American Drama* (Cambridge: Cambridge University Press, 1984), 2:56–57. Vivienne Dickson studies this and other manuscripts in the evolution of *Streetcar,* in *"A Streetcar Named Desire:* Its Development through the Manuscripts," in Tharpe, *Tennessee Williams,* 154–71.

12. MS., Humanities Research Center. Quoted in Bigsby, *Critical Introduction,* 58.

13. Brown, "Interview," 275.

14. Johan Huizinga, *Homo Ludens: A Study of the Play-Element in Culture* (London: Routledge and Kegan Paul, 1949), 132.

15. Robert Brustein, "America's New Culture Hero," in *A Streetcar Named Desire: Modern Critical Interpretations,* ed. Harold Bloom (New York: Chelsea House, 1988), 9–10.

16. Harold Clurman, "Tennessee Williams," *The Divine Pastime: Theatre Essays* (New York: Macmillan, 1974), 12–13.

17. Eric Bentley,"A Streetcar Named Desire," *In Search of Theatre* (New York: Vintage Books, 1959), 84.

18. Cohn, *Dialogue,* 106.

19. Mary McCarthy, "A Streetcar Called Success," *Sights and Spectacles, 1937–1956* (New York: Farrar, Straus, Cudahy, 1956), 133.

20. Frank Rich, "Alec Baldwin Does Battle with the Ghosts," *New York Times,* 13 April 1992, C11, 18.

21. Tennessee Williams, *Memoirs* (Garden City, N.Y.: Doubleday, 1975), 231.

CHAPTER FOUR

Summer and Smoke

Set in a small Southern town in the days before World War I, *Summer and Smoke* dramatizes the sexual awakening of Alma, a repressed young woman whose inner conflict between flesh and spirit is resolved with surprising consequences. The dichotomy between body and soul is reflected in the characters, action, language, symbolism, and setting of the play. Daughter of a straitlaced minister, Alma since childhood has felt an affinity with the statue of an angel, which stands in the town square as a drinking fountain, "brooding over the course of the play." The angel's cold stone and the life-giving water that springs from her hands symbolize the two opposing sides of Alma, whose name in Spanish means "soul"; although she appears icy, there is also "flame, mistaken for ice," as John, the man she loves, is to recognize too late.

The contrasts within Alma define the structure of the play. It is divided into two halves, "Summer," which the colder, "soul" aspect of Alma dominates, and "Winter," in which she comes to realize that body and soul both are necessary to attain eternity, the name of the statue. Also symbolizing the contrast between body and soul is the set, with the medical office on one side of the stage and the rectory on the other. The anatomy chart dominates John's office as the Angel of Eternity dominates the square.

In a series of encounters that increase in intensity, John, whom Alma has loved since they were children, challenges Alma's one-sided view of love as the soul's aspiration toward eternity, symbolized by the statue. His own equally narrow interpretation of love is a matter of the body, as symbolized by the anatomy chart. With poignant irony, the spiritual side of Alma's double nature (diagnosed by Dr. John as a "doppelganger") is in the ascendant when he is seeking physical gratification, and then "the tables [are] turned with a vengeance!"

Although Benjamin Nelson complains that the leading characters "are severely limited as human beings and everything they say emanates from the single point of view that each represents,"[1] Williams obviously intends Alma and John to be, like Chaucer's "humour" characters, defined by one overriding passion. Thus, they speak to us so directly in this work, which is clearly not naturalistic, though the original production offered no help to Williams's concept, which he outlines in the "Author's Production Notes" preceding the printed text.

The short story from which the play is developed sheds some light on the style of the drama. Like none of Williams's other stories on which he bases plays, "The Yellow Bird" (1947) begins in reality and proceeds to fantasy that is allegorical. Heroine Alma, daughter of a minister of Puritan descent, goes from repression to bizarre wildness as a reincarnation of Bobo, a yellow bird who had plagued her

SUMMER AND SMOKE

Puritan ancestor with lascivious suggestions while he was preaching. In the play, when the adult Alma first enters, she is "dressed in pale yellow and carries a yellow silk parasol," and Williams notes that "her true nature is still hidden even from herself." He portrays his heroine in delicate details. Although his technique is different from that of *Streetcar,* both chronicle the breakdown of a sensitive, generous human being. In a study of dramas reflecting Freudian theories W. David Sievers finds in Alma a "revealing portrait of the hysterical repression of sex into conversion symptoms in the South which to Williams symbolizes the last stronghold of unrealistic, ostrich-attitudes." [2]

Summer and Smoke begins with a brief prologue, depicting the two principals as children, Alma serious and caring and John happy-go-lucky, kissing her and running off. Introduced here are the motifs of eternity, the statue's nearly obliterated name, and death, John's aversion to his dead mother. A pattern of action is established which will be echoed in future scenes: John makes a physical advance and departs, leaving Alma "hurt and bewildered." In scene 1 a Fourth of July celebration is under way in the square as the adult Alma enters just after singing a solo with the town band. Williams describes her "self-consciousness . . . nervous laughter . . . . delicacy and elegance" and grace. Alma tells John, home from medical school and working with his doctor-father, that she suffers from "nervous heart trouble" and that his father next door is a great comfort to her. John's diagnosis is more down-to-earth: she is "swallowing air. . . . It's a little trick that hysterical women get into. . . . and it presses on your heart and gives you palpitations. That isn't serious in itself but it's a symptom of something that is. . . . Well, what I think you have is a *doppelganger!*" She is unaware of the word's meaning ("double person"), nor will he tell her, but this duality will be central to her character as the play develops.

When the fireworks begin (a recurring Williams symbol for sexual climax), John embarks on a series of physical contacts with Alma which will intensify in succeeding scenes until the "tables [are] turned."

> ALMA: There goes the first sky-rocket! Oh, look at it burst into a million stars!

> *(John leans way back to look up and allows his knees to spread wide apart so that one of them is in contact with Alma's. The effect upon her is curiously disturbing.)*

In an "emotional outburst" at the end of which she weeps, Alma upbraids John for his wild behavior, which dissipates his "gift for scientific research": "You have a chance to serve humanity. Not just to go on enduring for the sake of endurance." John "catches her hand" and "holds onto it." He invites Alma to go riding some afternoon but abruptly departs, pursuing Rosa Gonzales, who has appeared on the scene. In contrast to Alma's name, Rosa's symbolizes passion, one of the many associations of the rose in Williams's plays. Alma is so shattered by John's advances, which would be normal and predictable to anyone except her, that, when her friend Roger appears, she takes his arm (he being no physical threat): "I'll have to hang on your arm—I'm feeling so dizzy!" As the scene ends, "There is a final skyrocket. . . . and there is light on the angel."

After John has made a brief appearance at Alma's disastrous literary evening, their next encounter is in scene 4 at 2 A.M., when Alma comes to the office asking for John's father because she is "seriously ill." Williams delicately develops the physical tensions on John's part and the emotional strain on Alma's. First, John shows Alma his wound, just received in a fight, then suggests he check her heart—unbuttoning her blouse when she cannot (her fingers being "frozen"), diagnosing what he hears as "a little voice saying: 'Miss Alma is lonesome!'" and turning from the professional to the personal when "he lifts her hand from the chair arm" and asks, "What is this stone?" (a conventional approach to hand-holding.) "Fingers still frozen? . . . (*He lifts her hand to his mouth and blows his breath on her fingers.*)" John confesses, "Many's the time I've looked across at the Rectory and wondered if it would be worth trying, you and me," and makes a date with her for "Saturday night at eight o'clock." After Alma leaves John embraces the waiting Rosa, indicating his strong physical needs and foreshadowing the events in the arbor in scene 6.

The crucial arbor scene, lyric in tone, mounts inevitably to an emotional and physical climax. It takes place at the Moon Lake Casino and concludes the first half of the play, "Summer," which will contrast with "Winter," the second half. The Moon Lake Casino, where Blanche's young husband committed suicide after they drank and danced, is one of Williams's recurring symbols. To the obvious Freudian implications of the Moon Lake (scene of one of Amanda's beaux's drowning, Maggie's and Brick's deer hunting, and Lady's paternal wine garden) Williams adds the idea of the Casino, or chance, where one may hazard one's heart and lose, as do Blanche and Alma. John brings Alma to the Casino (her destination with another escort in the final scene), but she refuses to enter. She continues to upbraid him about his wildness and aimlessness, insisting that there is "more":

> Have you ever seen, or looked at a picture, of a Gothic cathedral? . . . How everything reaches up, how everything seems to be straining for something out of the reach of stone—or human—fingers? . . . [Williams's ellipsis]The immense stained windows, the great arched doors that are five or six times the height of the tallest man—the vaulted ceiling and all the delicate spires—all reaching up to something

beyond attainment! To me—well, that is the secret, the principle back of existence—the everlasting struggle and aspiration for more than our human limits have placed in our reach.

The Freudian imagery and the breathless climax of the speech reveal Alma's subliminal, physical yearning for John, her "true nature . . . still hidden even from herself," the flame beneath the ice. Williams humorously brings the scene back to earth as she concludes with a quotation, learns it is from Oscar Wilde, and is "somewhat taken aback" but recovers: "regardless . . . it's still true." Still rapt, she "places her hand over his." Significantly, it is she who makes the first physical move in this scene, but it is automatic, not deliberate. She is wearing gloves, in themselves a sign of her ladylike demeanor but also a symbol, a small but significant impediment to their physical contact. John remarks, "It's no fun holding hands with gloves on, Miss Alma." Alma removes her gloves and recounts her few "serious" dates, three young men in all, "and with each one there was a desert between us. . . . None of them really engaged my serious feelings."

> JOHN: You do have serious feelings—of that kind?
> ALMA: Doesn't everyone—sometimes?
> JOHN: Some women are cold. Some women are what is called frigid.

ALMA: Do I give that impression?

JOHN: Under the surface you have a lot of excitement, a great deal more than any other woman I have met. . . . The question is why? (*He leans over and lifts her veil.*)

ALMA: What are you doing that for?

JOHN: So that I won't get your veil in my mouth when I kiss you.

He kisses her, and kisses again, until "she hesitantly touches his shoulders, but not quite to push him away. John speaks softly to her": "Is it so hard to forget you're a preacher's daughter?"

But, at this point, Alma's inhibitions are too great. There is more to the "intimate relations" John finds necessary, she argues: "Some people bring just their bodies. But there are some people, there are some women, John—who can bring their hearts to it, also—who can bring their souls to it!"

John challenges her to find the soul on the chart of human anatomy in his office. A cock fight is beginning, and John invites her to watch it. She refuses.

JOHN: I know something else we could do. There are rooms above the Casino. . . . [Williams's ellipsis]

ALMA: What made you think I might be amenable to such a suggestion?

SUMMER AND SMOKE

JOHN: I counted your pulse in the office. . . .
ALMA: I was ill and went to your father for help.
JOHN: It was me you went to. . . . Fingers frozen
stiff when I . . . [Williams's ellipsis]

At this point, realizing the truth of John's recollection, Alma, unable to face that truth, "hysterically" demands a taxi. John rushes off to call one, as Alma repeats, "*(wildly) You're not a gentleman!*"

When Alma speaks of John's gift for scientific research and of the higher aims to which he should be dedicating himself, she may be voicing his own sense of guilt and betrayal hidden beneath his wild behavior. An awareness of this on the part of the actor (though not evidenced in the productions here discussed) would make more credible John's sudden turnabout from self-indulgent sensualist to serious scientist. For just as Alma will change in "Winter" from her role as "preacher's daughter" and shed the inhibitions the small town has imposed upon her, so John will abandon his role of devil-may-care man-about-town and dedicate himself to science. John's sudden transformation can be convincing if the actor is skillful enough, for events move swiftly and melodramatically in scenes 7 and 8. Notified by phone of John's wild party, his father bursts in and is fatally shot by Rosa's father, who owns the casino. To settle his gambling debts there, John has agreed to marry Rosa.

UNDERSTANDING TENNESSEE WILLIAMS

Learning in the next scene that it was Alma's phone call that brought his father home, John upbraids her as a "white-blooded spinster," points to the anatomy chart, insisting that along with the brain which is hungry for truth and the belly which is hungry for food, one has to feed "the sex which is hungry for love because it is sometimes lonesome." Alma responds, "—I reject your opinion of where love is," and insists that the soul is there, "not seen, but there": "And it's *that* that I loved you with—that! Not what you mention!—Yes, did love you with, John, did nearly *die* of when you hurt me!"

Except in these two scenes, in which there is perhaps too much action, there is little elsewhere. All of the drama in the duologues between Alma and John is in the conflict between the characters and within themselves. In the final scenes Williams employs lyricism, symbolism, and emotion rather than action to bring the play to a climax and its surprising though inevitable conclusion.

While Alma's "cold" self dominates "Summer," we see a different Alma in the second half of the play, "Winter." Just as the seasons change, so does Alma; her summer "coolness"—too late—has become heat by winter. Alma tells John in their final encounter in scene 11: "The girl who said 'no,' she doesn't exist any more, she died last summer,— suffocated in smoke from something on fire inside her."

Alma arrives at the surgery, just as she did earlier, only now the physical advances are hers (she is unaware that John is engaged to Nellie). John, asking if she has been

SUMMER AND SMOKE

"anxious" about her heart, counts her pulse. Alma responds, "And now the stethoscope?" He "starts to loosen her jacket. . . . Slowly, involuntarily, her gloved hands lift and descend on the crown of his head. He gets up awkwardly. She suddenly leans toward him and presses her mouth to his."

But now John tells Alma that he has "come around to your way of thinking, that something else is in there, an immaterial something—as thin as smoke. . . . and knowing it's there—why, then the whole thing—this—this unfathomable experience of ours—takes on a whole new value." When Alma asks him, "Why didn't it happen between us?" he replies that in the "three or four times that we've—come face to face. . . . we seemed to be trying to find something in each other without knowing what it was we wanted to find. . . . It wasn't the physical you that I really wanted! . . . You didn't have that to give me. . . . You had something else to give. . . . You couldn't name it and I couldn't recognize it. I thought it was just a Puritanical ice that glittered like flame. But now I believe it *was* flame, mistaken for ice."

In Alma's response Williams employs such poetic devices as alliteration, assonance, balance, and quaint, everyday imagery to achieve a poignant, emotional effect:

The tables have turned with a vengeance! You've come around to my old way of thinking and I to yours like two people exchanging a call on each other at the same time, and each one finding the other gone out, the door locked against him and no one to answer the bell! I came here to tell you that being a gentleman doesn't seem so important to me any more, but you're telling me I've got to remain a lady.

Williams is one of the few American playwrights to create dialogue that is unique and personal to a particular character. Amanda, Blanche, Stanley, Alma, Big Daddy—each has an idiom that is identifiably hers or his alone. Williams considered himself a "lyric" playwright, recognizing that his dialogue was artistic, not realistic. Some of his technique of speech as poetry reflects T. S. Eliot's theory of poetry as speech.[3]

Alma's locutions are described to her by John as "a rather fancy way of talking. . . . 'pyrotechnical display' instead of fireworks, and that sort of thing. . . . And how about that accent?" Alma replies, "I have sometimes been accused of having a put-on accent by people who disapprove of good diction."

At their first meeting as adults Alma's lengthy opening speech to John chooses a conventional topic, the weather, but its diction and rhythms are characteristically Alma's:

Summer is not the pleasantest time of year to renew an acquaintance with Glorious Hill—is it? The Gulf wind has failed us this year, disappointed us dreadfully this summer. We used to be able to rely on the Gulf wind to cool the nights off for us, but this summer has been an exceptional season. . . . There, the Gulf wind is stirring! He's actually moving the leaves of the palmetto! And listen to them complaining . . . . [Williams's ellipsis]

Williams here uses personification, alliteration, and, in the last two sentences, onomatopoeia, combining and repeating *s* sibilants and *t* plosives to reproduce the sound of the wind blowing and the palmetto leaves "complaining." More than once the playwright remarked that poetry need not be confined to formal verse and might well be expressed in plays.

Alma's speech is in keeping with the character as Williams introduces her in the stage directions in scene 1: "In Alma's voice and manner there is a delicacy and elegance. . . . Her gestures and mannerisms are a bit exaggerated but in a graceful way." Her way of speaking demonstrates Williams's observation that "her true nature is still hidden even from herself." The use of the poetic rather than the realistic word, the euphemistic rather than the down-to-earth, reflects Alma's protective covering, also evident in her ladylike demeanor and the hat and gloves with which she holds reality at arm's length. The "Puritanical ice" conceals "flame, mistaken for ice," but by the time she and John realize this it is too late.

Alma's predicament conforms with Robert Heilman's definition of tragedy as "polypathic," in which the audience experiences "the conflicting impulses of the divided man," as opposed to melodrama, which is "monopathic," in which there is a "oneness of feeling," the hero is not divided, not in conflict over opposing alternatives.[4] Diagnosed by John in scene 1 as having a doppelganger, Alma recognizes in their final scene together that, in contrast to John's "single-ness," she is "weak and divided," one of those "who slip like shadows among you solid strong ones." She is the more complex of the two, and the ice-fire conflict within her evokes sympathy; while an audience may pity her unrewarded love for John, they might respond to him with impatience.

It is characteristic of the playwright not to employ a predictable ending, with Alma's face "bathed in tears" as she leaves the surgery with her prescription while John "rains kisses on Nellie's forehead and throat and lips." For Williams has magic up his sleeve. Although Signi Falk prudishly calls the ending "improbable and grotesque,"[5] in as finely sprung a character as Alma's tension must be followed by release. The final scene is a dramatic coup, as the action is carried to its poetic conclusion, or its Freudian inevitability (as "sex comes too violently after too long a period of suppression"),[6] and Alma's sexual awakening drives her into the arms of a stranger. With the Angel of Eternity still brooding over the action, the salesman echoes the end of the arbor scene, calling "Taxi"; this time Alma will ascend to the rooms upstairs.

The symbols representing Alma—the statue of the Angel of Eternity, the fountain of water (purifying, life-giving), winter-summer, fire beneath the Puritanical ice—all serve to strengthen an impression of her cold exterior hiding an interior flame that matches and even exceeds the passion of John. But to indicate that in *Summer and Smoke* Williams creates symbols that have as their rationale "progressive insanity" [7] is to go too far. Alma's doppelganger is hardly insanity but more a truth about life, that the seeming cold may be hiding fire inside. It is Alma's mother who is mentally unstable, who, as Alma reveals in scene 1, "started slipping back into her childhood" as soon as her husband was ordained, "to escape the responsibilities of a rectory." In scene 10 Alma tells busybody Mrs. Bassett that her gossip has been overheard: "I haven't been very well, but—I am not—as you put it—'going the way Mother went.'"

In evading her responsibilities and forcing them on Alma, her mother has deprived her of a normal childhood and womanhood: "People. . . . pity me—think of me as an old maid already!" she accuses her mother in scene 2. "In spite of I'm young. Still young! It's you—it's you, you've taken my youth away from me!" Alma, as Louise Blackwell points out, has "multiple roles to play," that of daughter and hostess for her minister father and sister and parent to her mother, with "no role that she desires for herself." [8] Inhibiting Alma are not only family tensions but also the expectations of 1916 Southern small-town society, which defined idealistically rather than realistically the role of a "preacher's daughter" and the behavior of a "lady." In this respect Alma resembles Amanda and Blanche who, notes Nada Zeineddine, are "alienated from a tenable life within themselves and their societies by their moral illusions of their own purity and innocence." She notes that "a concern with the flesh-spirit duality . . . runs through Williams's plays, and characterizes his vision of life." [9]

Throughout *Summer and Smoke* its setting, characters, and theme are reminders of the dichotomy between the spirit and the flesh. When the curtain rises the Winemiller rectory parlor on one side of the stage and the Buchanan doctor's office on the other represent the spiritual and physical struggle within Alma as well as the division between body and soul which John and she personify. *A Debate between Body and Soul* was one of the earliest of the medieval morality plays; it has been noted above that Alma and John are like "humour" characters of that period, and her speech on Gothic cathedrals and his on the anatomy chart resemble contrasting sides of such a debate.

The division of the play into Summer and Winter, the seasons of the action, also suggests the two opposing aspects of Alma, ice and flame. Although the statue named Eternity is of cold stone, the life-giving water of its fountain suggests Williams's theme that love that includes both soul and body is a means to eternity. Alma's "ice" character of part 1 will "flame" in part 2, just as the earlier, wild John becomes the serious John in part 2. As the play progresses, each will "recognize within himself what he has seen and reached for in the other," Gerald Weales points out.[10] But the recognition is badly timed, as Alma reflects in her wistful simile of social callers who miss one another at their respective homes. This "symmetry of reversals" at the end, Heilman notes, is reminiscent of Ibsen's *Rosmersholm,* "where Rebecca West comes to believe in Rosmer's ideal of nobility, while Rosmer loses faith in his mission to ennoble men." [11]

Humor is never absent from a Williams play; he once observed, "I make some serious, even tragic observations about society, but I make them through the medium of comedy." [12] He considered his humor "Gothic" and claims to have invented American black (serious) comedy.[13] In scene 3 the literary society meeting is an ironically humorous expose of narrow-minded, gossiping villagers whose pretentious literary aspirations collapse when Blake, confused with Dowson, is accused of being "immoral."

Although the ending of *Summer and Smoke* is less theatrical than that of *Streetcar,* the sense of loss is as great: a finely wrought, sensitive, vulnerable woman here realizes her true nature too late and veers from one extreme to the other, led by a "stranger" along a destructive path. The feeling of loss which pervades the ending of these two plays also is felt at the final curtain of *The Glass Menagerie.* In the draft of an unpublished article among his papers at the University of Texas, Williams mentions that he thought of the three plays as "a trio . . . which embodied a single theme, or legend, that of the delicate, haunted girl who first appeared as Laura, the basic theme of the over-sensitive misfit in a world that spins with blind fury." [14]

Appearing a year after the great success of *A Streetcar Named Desire,* with its vivid colors of van Gogh's *All Night Cafe, Summer and Smoke* painted its portraits in pastels. The critics were less than enthusiastic. Brooks Atkinson, whose *New York Times* reviews dictated box office success or failure, found the play "a tone poem in the genre of *The Glass Menagerie* and *A Streetcar Named Desire* . . . the same mystic frustration and the same languid doom": "So far Mr. Williams has been writing variations on the same theme" (7 October l948). The review met with a barrage of letters to the Sunday section of the *Times,* charging the critic with failure to recognize poetic theater when he saw it. Harold Clurman in the *New Republic* was unenthusiastic as well: "So much time is given to a conscious exposition of theme that Williams loses the specific sense of his people and to a dangerous extent our concern as spectators . . . the play alternates between psychoanalytic 'hints' . . . and what becomes . . . an almost trite and badly-constructed plot line" (25 October l948).

Opening on Broadway so soon after the debut of *Streetcar, Summer and Smoke,* Broadway pundits alleged, was "pulled out of the trunk," that is, was written earlier but now rushed into production to capitalize on the earlier success. Actually, Williams had worked on the two plays simultaneously. Margo Jones, who ran a successful regional theater in Dallas, had produced the play there, gained the rights, and insisted on producing and directing it on Broadway. The direction, acting, and set could be most kindly described as inadequate and out of tune with the play, which is set in a minor key. Williams himself confesses: "Now you may think, perhaps correctly, that I am a total ingrate when I say that in my opinion Margo Jones should have confined herself to a regional theater, preferably in the executive and fund-raising departments. But I think it was there that her genius lay, not in the direction of actors or of delicate plays." [15]

In his "Author's Production Notes" Williams calls for a much less realistic set than was seen in the Broadway production. He cites modern artist Giorgio De Chirico's use (in *Conversation among the Ruins*) of "fragmentary walls and interiors in a very evocative way" and says he would like all three locales—town square, rectory, and doctor's office—"to form an harmonious whole like one complete picture rather than three separate ones." The actual set turned out to be the latter rather than the former. The statue of the Angel, "a symbolic figure (Eternity) brooding over the course of the play," was much too large, set squarely in the middle, with realistic interiors of Alma's house and the doctor's office on either side, rather than "fragmentary walls and interiors." Although Williams states that "an imaginative designer may solve these plastic problems in a variety of ways and should not feel bound by any of my specific suggestions," in actuality Williams's original designers too often revealed a lack of imagination, creating realistic settings at odds with the spirit of the plays.

Throughout his career Williams suffered psychologically from unfavorable reviews, especially those of Brooks Atkinson of the *Times,* who said of *Summer and Smoke:* "Mr. Williams is full of scorn for the rootless people he pities. He will not raise a finger to help them" (7 October 1948). One wonders to what extent Atkinson, whose experience was in theory of theater rather than practice, recognized the script beneath the bad production. At that time Walter Kerr and Harold Clurman were the only major critics who had had practical, professional stage experience. Richard Watts of the *New York Post* was obviously reacting to the performances rather than to the script when he observed, "While its hero and heroine think and talk a lot about sex and passion, there is an almost academic quality about their preoccupations" (7 October 1948).

Four years later the critics were more receptive to the play, which was revived off Broadway, directed by Jose Quintero in a sensitive, moving production that realized the poetic values of the work. It introduced Geraldine Page as Alma in a performance so luminous, so right in each small detail as well as in the larger outline, that she was known thereafter as a "Williams actor," her later roles including the female lead in *Sweet Bird of Youth.*

The 1961 Paramount film, directed by Peter Glenville, preserves Miss Page's brilliantly delineated interpretation of Alma, although from time to time her stage gestures are too large when magnified on the screen. She disclosed later that she virtually repeated her off-Broadway performance, for she had not been advised to scale down her technique for her first screen role. It is the only film version of a serious Williams play filmed within a decade of its major production (Quintero's) which does not change the ending to a happy one. Faithfulness to the text, Miss Page's acting, and that of Una Merkel as Alma's childish mother are other advantages that make the film version a definitive one.

For the November 1951 London premiere Williams states that, in Rome during the preceding summer, he wrote a revised version, called *The Eccentricities of a Nightingale.* But he arrived in England too late to substitute the rewritten script, as the original version was already in rehearsal and would have a brief run.[16] In his "Author's Note" to the texts of the two plays, published in 1964, Williams feels that *Eccentricities* "is a better work than the play from which it is derived."

The major change is in the character of Alma. In *Nightingale* she never keeps her love for John hidden. She is the one who asks if there are places they can go to, to be alone, even for an hour. They do go, even though John says he doesn't love her; her response is that an hour will be enough for her. At first the room is cold, their efforts to light a fire seem to fail, and they decide to leave. Then the fire springs to life, and John is about to kiss her when the scene ends; we assume they make love.

In this version Alma is a true "eccentric," not just someone who is "different," so that the exaggeration of both characteristics, her desire and her difference, makes Alma less dramatic by reducing the conflict within her. Mrs. Winemiller is more mad than in the earlier play, in which her arrested development made her childlike, a "cross to bear" for both Alma and her father. An addition that is hardly advantageous is John's fat, possessive mother, hostile to Alma and interfering in the couple's encounters. Obedient to his mother throughout, John is serious, never wild. The most important difference is that Alma and John *do* go upstairs. It is as if Williams felt an obligation to them and to the audience and to Brooks Atkinson and so supplied what everyone seemed to expect. But it is an artistic misjudgment that diminishes the poignant appeal of Alma's character. A television production of *Eccentricities* in June 1976 was well acted by Blythe Danner and Frank Langella as the principals, but it only bore out the consensus of thinking critics that Williams got it right the first time around.

Opening on Broadway so soon after *Streetcar,* and with an inferior production, *Summer and Smoke* originally suffered by comparison. Now *Summer and Smoke* can be appreciated for its originality of characterization, its poetry, and its poignancy. Alma joins the Williams galaxy of women whose characters are so completely delineated that they themselves become prototypes. After an acquaintance with this heroine one may better understand the "Almas . . . of this world,"[17] those who might be dismissed as eccentric had one not seen, with Williams as guide, into Alma's heart.

Notes

1. Benjamin Nelson, *Tennessee Williams: The Man and His Work* (New York: Ivan Obolensky, 1961), 126.

2. W. David Sievers, "Tennessee Williams and Arthur Miller," *Freud on Broadway: A History of Psychoanalysis and the American Drama* (New York: Cooper Square Publishers, 1955), 382.

3. Eliot's influence is discussed in chapter 6 (in my study of *Camino Real*).

4. Robert B. Heilman, *The Iceman, the Arsonist, and the Troubled Agent: Tragedy and Melodrama on the Modern Stage* (Seattle: University of Washington Press, 1973), 57–58.

5. Signi L. Falk, *Tennessee Williams* (New York: Twayne Publishers, 1961), 93.

6. Sievers, *Freud on Broadway,* 376.

7. Esther Merle Jackson, *The Broken World of Tennessee Williams* (Madison: University of Wisconsin Press, 1965), 48.

UNDERSTANDING TENNESSEE WILLIAMS

8. Louise Blackwell, "Tennessee Williams and the Predicament of Women," *South Atlantic Bulletin* 35 (March 1970): 10.

9. Nada Zeineddine, *Because It Is My Name* (Braunton and Devon, U.K.: Merlin Books, 1991), 136.

10. Gerald Weales, *Tennessee Williams* (Minneapolis: University of Minnesota Press, 1965), 39.

11. Heilman, *The Iceman,* 120.

12. Dotson Rader, "The Art of Theatre V: Tennessee Williams," in *Conversations with Tennessee Williams,* ed. Albert J. Devlin (Jackson: University Press of Mississippi, 1986), 355.

13. Tennessee Williams, *Memoirs* (Garden City, N.Y.: Doubleday, 1975), 212.

14. Quoted in C. W. E. Bigsby, *A Critical Introduction to Twentieth-Century American Drama* (Cambridge: Cambridge University Press, 1984), 2:70.

15. Williams, *Memoirs,* 153.

16. "I am perplexed at the shortness of the run. I suppose people just don't care enough about the Almas and Roses . . . of this world as they ought to, or I was not able to put it into sufficiently eloquent words to make them care that much," Williams wrote to Maria Britneva (in *Five O'Clock Angel: Letters of Tennessee Williams to Maria St. Just, 1948–1982,* ed. Maria St. Just [New York: Alfred A. Knopf, 1990], 54).

17. Ibid.

CHAPTER FIVE

The Rose Tattoo

The Rose Tattoo is a comedy celebrating elemental human passions—love, superstition, jealousy, possessiveness—set against a communal background of women and children as choral accompaniment. Williams describes the play as "the Dionysian element in human life, its mystery, its beauty, its significance." [1] As he sets the scene in his "Author's Production Notes," the opening curtain is orchestrated: "A Sicilian folk singer with a guitar" is heard, and the song will continue between the scenes, to be completed at the final curtain. The lighting is "extremely romantic," that of "late dusk," as a cutaway or transparency reveals the interior of a simple cottage in a Southern town along "the Gulf Coast between New Orleans and Mobile." Among the religious articles and pictures is a little statue of the Madonna with a vigil light. "Our purpose is to show these gaudy, childlike mysteries with sentiment and humor in equal measure, without ridicule and with respect for the religious yearnings they symbolize," states Williams. Also part of the interior is another "chorus" of mutes—seven dressmaker dummies. "The mothers . . . are beginning to call their children . . . in voices near and distant, urgent and tender, like the variable notes of wind and water." Musical sounds, both instrumental and vocal, are so important and the passions so elemental, the play might well serve as the libretto of an opera. In most of Williams's plays the forces of love battle the forces of death; in this joyous comedy love wins.

Serafina Delle Rose, the heroine of the play, is a Sicilian seamstress, earthy, possessive, and proud. Pregnant, dressed in pale rose silk, she is awaiting the return of her truck driver husband, Rosario, as the play opens. Her existence centers upon their marriage. As she is to recall in scene 5: "My husband was a Sicilian. We had love together every night of the week, we never skipped one, from the night we was married till the night he was killed in his fruit truck on that road there!"

This affirmation of sex, a tone that pervades *The Rose Tattoo,* reflects the influence of D. H. Lawrence. In the forenote to his one-act play *I Rise in Flame, Cried the Phoenix,* about the death of Lawrence, Williams observes: "Lawrence felt the mystery and power of sex, as the primal life urge, and was the . . . adversary of those who wanted to keep the subject locked away. . . . Much of his work is . . . distorted by tangent obsessions, such as his insistence upon the woman's subservience to the male, but all in all his work is probably the greatest modern monument to the dark roots of creation." [2]

In the opening scene Serafina's neighbor, who claims knowledge of the occult, learns that Serafina was aware of her present pregnancy "on the very night of conception" because she felt a stigmata on her breast and saw on it,

THE ROSE TATTOO

momentarily, the rose that was tattooed on the breast of her husband. Two short scenes follow. A mourning chorus of keening, black-shawled women bring news that Rosario is dead, and when his mistress Estelle appears they curse her. Then the doctor announces that Serafina has had a miscarriage.

In scene 4 the main action begins three years later and takes place within twenty-four hours. It is high school graduation day, and the chorus of women, now strident and insulting, bang the doors and shutters of Serafina's cottage, demanding the graduation dresses she has made for their daughters. Serafina, whose daughter also is graduating, has changed greatly: "She is wearing a soiled pink slip and her hair is wild." She is enraged when the women whisper of Rosario's infidelities with Estelle, who deals blackjack at the local casino. Serafina refuses to believe the gossip and is constantly entreating the statue of the Madonna for a "sign" that Rosario was true to her.

The structure is that of a visit. Truck driver Alvaro arrives upon the scene, and his developing relationship with Serafina will change her anger and suspicion to love and tolerance. In contrast to the seriocomic romance between Serafina and Alvaro is the intense young love blossoming between her daughter Rosa and Jack, a sailor she has met at the high school dance.

The first meeting of Serafina and Alvaro, in scene 1 of the second act, follows her altercation with the priest over

Rosario's infidelity, which Serafina has always denied. Against church doctrine she had had Rosario's body cremated and keeps the ashes in an urn before the statue of the Madonna. She insists that the priest, who heard Rosario's confession, confirm or discredit the rumor of infidelity, but he refuses to do either. "I will go mad with the doubt in my heart and I will smash the urn and scatter the ashes—of my husband's body!" she threatens, and, as the priest fearfully retreats, she turns to the Madonna, crying, "Give me a sign!"

"As if in mocking answer, a novelty salesman appears. . . . His entrance is accompanied by a brief, satiric strain of music." Then truck driver Alvaro enters, "with pent-up fury at a world of frustrations . . . localized in the gross figure of this salesman," who has insulted him on the road. They fight. The salesman viciously knees Alvaro in the groin and departs. The defeated man rushes into the cottage and begins to sob: "I got to cry after a fight. I'm sorry, lady." Serafina responds in kind: "I always cry— when somebody else is crying." When he takes off his torn jacket for her to mend, she exclaims to herself, "*My husband's body,* with the head of a *clown!*" With compassion and humor the rest of the play depicts their growing relationship.

Their first conversation "is full of odd hesitations, broken sentences and tentative gestures. . . . Their fumbling communication has a curious intimacy and sweetness, like the meeting of two lonely children for the first time." In keeping with Sicilian traditions of hospitality as well as with the play's "Bacchantic impulse," they drink wine. Polite questions arise, usual between a man and a woman at their first meeting to determine if the other is unattached.

> SERAFINA: I was a peasant, but I married a baron!—No, I still don't believe it! I married a baron when I didn't have shoes!
> ALVARO: Excuse me for asking—but where is the Baron, now? . . .
> SERAFINA: Them're his ashes in that marble urn.

Then they touch. As she will mend his torn shirt later, Serafina lends Alvaro the red silk shirt Estelle had ordered but never called for.

> ALVARO: There is nothing more beautiful than a gift between people!—Now you are smiling!—You like me a little bit better?
> SERAFINA: (*slowly and tenderly*): You know what they should of done when you was a baby? They should of put tape on your ears to hold them back so when you grow up they wouldn't stick out like the wings of a little kewpie! (*She touches his ear, a very slight touch, betraying too much of her heart.*)

A goat belonging to the Strega (believed to be a witch) breaks into Serafina's yard; Alvaro chases and catches him. Then he asks her name: "I got to go now,—You have been troppo gentile, Mrs. . . ." (Williams's ellipsis). Serafina answers: "I am the widow of the Baron Delle Rose.— Excuse the way I'm—not dressed . . . (*He keeps hold of her hand as he stands on the porch steps.)*" (Williams's ellipsis).

Williams states that the "lyric as well as the Bacchantic impulse" characterizes the play, and, as the scene ends, he lifts it to lyricism, as expressed by the clownish truck driver in monosyllables that are as rhythmic as his movements:

> ALVARO: The rose is the heart of the world like the heart is the—heart of the—body! But you, Baronessa . . . . You have put your heart in the marble urn with the ashes. . . . And if . . . sometime . . . the marble urn was to *break!* . . . Look! Look, Baronessa! . . . I was pointing at your heart, broken out of the urn and away from the ashes! . . . *(He whistles like a bird and makes graceful wing-like motions with his hands. . . . He imitates a bird flying off with gay whistles.)*
> SERAFINA: Buffone!

The character of Serafina dominates *The Rose Tattoo*. She is tough and realistic, but at the same time vulnerable and romantic in her notions of love and religion. Above all, she is passionate in everything she does, whether she is locking her daughter in the house to keep her from Jack ("We are Sicilians. We don't leave the girls with the boys they're not engaged to!" she tells him in act 1) or destroying the urn and breaking her ties with Rosario and the Madonna. As she is tempestuous and variable, it is no surprise when her devotion to the dead Rosario veers to the opposite extreme. In scene 1 of the third act, after her phone conversation with Estelle, Serafina, now convinced of Rosario's unfaithfulness, breaks the urn and blows out the Madonna's votive light: "I don't believe in you, Lady! . . . I forget you the way you forget Serafina!" As the scene ends, she encourages the returning Alvaro: "Now we can go on with our—conversation." She is entirely convincing and sympathetic as she changes from a wife whose life centers upon marital love to a ferocious yet despondent widow, to an emotionally charged expectant lover who again becomes pregnant. In each stage, unlike Blanche and Alma, she knows herself.

As the play is Williams's version of a celebration of Dionysus, which he characterizes as "the homely light of a kitchen candle burned in praise of a god," so his heroine, like her classical predecessors, arrives at a truth through suffering: "It took an almost literal unclothing, a public appearance in a wine-stained rayon slip, a fierce attack on a priest and the neighbor women, to learn that the blood of the wild young daughter was better, as a memorial, than ashes kept in a crematory urn," says Williams.[3] In his study of modern plays that combine both tragic and comic elements, J. L. Styan suggests that *The Rose Tattoo* might be so classified. Serafina's "sin of pride" regarding Rosario might be tragic in another context, he notes, but the emotion contrasts with the "incongruous details of her ordinary life," which provoke comedy.[4]

In some ways the play resembles Lorca's tragedy *Yerma,* in a version that is resolved comically. There is the chorus of women who keen at the death of Rosario and who gossip about Serafina, there is mystery and superstition, and there is the yearning for a child—here fulfilled by a clownish stranger whom the village celebrates. Lorca-like, Williams develops the play in a series of conflicts between protagonist and antagonist, while the chorus comments. Lorca's plays were popular on New York stages off Broadway at the time Williams was writing *The Rose Tattoo,* and in his one-act verse tragedy *The Purification* his debt to the Spanish playwright is evident. When Williams attended Washington University in St. Louis in the 1930s, among the modern writers he admired and who would later influence him were Lorca, Lawrence, and Hart Crane.[5]

Williams's ending is celebratory, its merriment drawn in the bold, comic strip fashion of a Lorca comedy such as *The Love of Don Perlimplín.* Serafina rejects death for life, abstinence for love (for Rosa as well as herself), isolation for the community, and barrenness for pregnancy. In a communal celebration, as the women pass Rosario's red silk shirt (now Alvaro's) along from hand to hand, Serafina starts up the embankment and calls to Alvaro, "Vengo, vengo, amore! (*and the curtain falls as the music rises with her in great glissandi of sound.)*"

Signi Falk, who characterizes Serafina as a "Southern wench," deplores that the play is "overlaid with a tragic mood and pathos; with comedy and low farce; with rhetorical outbursts; and, at times, even with obscenity." She finds "as many erotic symbols as Williams could crowd into one play. There is some rather beautiful dialogue; but the play also has some of the usual rhetoric and regrettably adolescent vulgarity."[6]

That symbols abound in the play is true, but they are much more varied than "erotic." Some of the symbols used and understood by the characters are, like them, drawn in clear, bold strokes: the roses, the Madonna, fire, heat, the goat, and the red silk shirt. Others are commonplace objects that take on added significance in this context—like the wristwatch, the dressmaker dummies, and the rose tattoo.

A symbol of love and life since ancient times, the rose permeates the Delle Rose household; its profusion as symbol reflects the excesses of the characters. Husband and child are Rosario and Rosa; in the opening scene roses are in Serafina's hair, in a bowl, and printed on the wallpaper and carpet. Rosario has a rose tattooed on his chest, wears rose oil on his hair, and is to receive a rose-colored shirt ordered by Estelle.

Both the heat of the day and the heat of passion are reflected in Alvaro's approach to Serafina in act 3:

> ALVARO: (*He stretches the palms of his hands out toward her as if she were a fireplace in a freezing-cold room.*) The night is warm but I feel like my hands are—freezing!
> SERAFINA: Bad—circulation . . . [Williams's ellipsis]
> ALVARO: No, too *much* circulation! . . . Across the room I feel the sweet warmth of a lady! . . . I know that's what warms the world, that is what makes it the summer!

The goat, a symbol of lust since classical times, here is a pesky animal belonging to the feared Strega, who "shook hands with the devil" and has the "evil eye," as does the goat: "He got in my yard the night that I lost Rosario and my boy!" laments Serafina in act 2. When Alvaro captures the goat at the end of the act he enters in a mock-heroic triumphal procession, followed by the children clapping tin lids together like cymbals.

The dressmaker's dummies, representing the seven ages, transform the commonplace into a world stage. Williams directs in his "Author's Production Notes" that the seven dummies "will have to be made especially for the play as their purpose is not realistic." Unlike armless, headless, real dressmaker dummies, these "life-size mannequins . . . . have pliable joints so that their positions can be changed. Their arms terminate at the wrist. In all their attitudes there is an air of drama, somewhat like the poses of declamatory actresses of the old school." But they are only dummies, not human beings. When Serafina is despondent after her encounter with two vindictive "female clowns," she is found by Rosa in scene 6 of act 1 "slumped in a chair. . . . grotesquely surrounded by the dummies, as though she had been holding a silent conference with them." Alienated from the community, she can relate only to dummies, which, says Williams, "eventually . . . must be knocked over, however elaborate their trappings."[7]

In contrast to the women of the neighborhood, the dummies form their own chorus—bloodless personifications of the seven stages of life and a reminder, as is the wristwatch, of the relentless passage of time. The young girl (who wears "a girlish frock . . . an Alice-blue gown with daisies crocheted on it") will one day be a bride. The bridal gown dummy wears "a net gown . . . trimmed in white satin—lustrous, immaculate," but one day she will be a widow, like the dummy in a costume "complete from black-veiled hat to black slippers." The latter two, indicate the production notes, "face each other in violent attitudes, as though having a shrill argument." They are visual embodiments of Williams's recurring theme of desire and death, in this play Rosario's and the baby's deaths leading to transcendence through the new life created by Serafina's liaison with Alvaro.

Four rose tattoos (including Serafina's vision) would seem excessive in any other context, but here they match the exuberance of the play and the characters. As a flower, the rose symbolizes love and life, but, as a tattoo, it evokes humor and reflects the comic exaggeration that infuses the play. The stately courtiers and symbolic roses of medieval tapestries and literature such as *The Romance of the Rose* are linked, through the rose tattoo, with the earthy Sicilian truck drivers and laborers of a run-down Gulf town. As in the medieval romance, the rose (tattoo) marks the point at which the plot turns. In scene 1 of act 3, when Estelle confirms Rosario's infidelity (". . . if you think I'm a liar, come here and let me show you his rose tattooed on my chest!"), Serafina rejects the dead and accepts Alvaro, who has had a rose tattooed on his chest in the interval between the invitation and the assignation. The rose's mystic associations, as Chaucer treats them, are here evident in Serafina's "seeing" momentarily a rose tattoo on her breast as a sign that she has conceived.

While symbolism and nonrealistic stage effects abound, the dialogue gives a surface impression of actual speech, but it is speech heightened and sharpened by Williams to give it depth and humor. He creates for Serafina an idiom that is uniquely hers—tough, wisecracking, repetitive, rhythmic, grammatically unstructured, and reverting from English to Italian (the latter almost always easily understood by the audience).

Her sentences are simple and short, her vocabulary limited and reiterative, but the words, rhythms, and repetition become poetic, a reminder of the "lyric" Dionysus. In scene 5 of act 1 she tells the "man-crazy" Bessie and Flora of her true love for Rosario: "I count up the nights I held him all night in my arms, and I can tell you how many. Each night for twelve years. Four thousand—three hundred—and eighty. The number of nights I held him all night in my arms. Sometimes I didn't sleep, just held him all night in my arms. And I am satisfied with it. I grieve for him."

For Serafina everyday English words take on literal meanings: "How high is this high school?" she asks the teacher. Or when she meets Jack in scene 6, act 1:

> SERAFINA: Hun-ter?
> JACK: Yes, ma'am, Hunter. Jack Hunter.
> SERAFINA: What are you hunting?—Jack? . . .
> What all of 'em are hunting?

Sometimes she rises to simple lyricism: "A man, when he burns, leaves only a handful of ashes. No woman can hold him. The wind must blow him away."[8]

Much of the play's humor is to be found in her realistic, down-to-earth remarks. Her interview with Jack in scene 6 recalls Lady Bracknell's querying another Jack in *The Importance of Being Earnest:*

> SERAFINA: What are you? Catholic?
> JACK: Me? Yes, ma'am, Catholic.
> SERAFINA: You don't look Catholic to me! . . . Turn around, will you?
> JACK: Do what, ma'am?
> SERAFINA: I said, *turn around!* . . . Why do they make them Navy pants so tight?

Comedy figures in all Williams's plays, even the tragedies, but here it is all-pervading, sustaining throughout a Bacchantic tone. Not only is there verbal humor, especially in Serafina's dialogue, but all the devices of comedy are to be found in the action. Physical farce abounds, with chases inside the house (Alvaro and Serafina) and outside (Alvaro and the goat). Serafina's ample build traps her on a chair as she reaches for wine, and it defeats her in a struggle with her girdle. In the third scene of act 3, when Alvaro enters with his eyes "barely open" and his legs "rubbery," to discover Rosa asleep on the couch, Williams directs that the scene be played with "the pantomimic lightness, almost fantasy, of an early Chaplin comedy."

In another context Serafina's hyperbole would be absurd; here it accords with her larger-than-life character.

"Buffone" is her description of Alvaro, the clumsy, oafish buffoon at whose discomfort audiences, secure in their superiority, have tolerantly laughed since Roman days. A wooing scene that is a comedy of errors, including presentation of candy rejected by a former sweetheart, reaches a hilarious climax when Alvaro drops the condom. Bessie and Flora, described by Serafina as "female clowns," are hardly "prostitutes," as Styan believes but, rather, satirical portraits of a particular type of garrulous Southern woman whom Williams describes as man-crazy and for whom a veterans' convention is an excuse for women as well as men to shed any and all inhibitions.

As is true of all Williams's plays, the world of this play is unique, and, just as he creates a total poetic environment that blends lighting, setting, properties, costumes, and score (including both music and sound effects), so are the characters of this little Gulf town individual to their play and to their play alone. The speech patterns of everyone in *The Rose Tattoo,* from Serafina to the Strega, exactly fit not only the speaker but the time and the locale. And when we consider that the speeches are heightened, and not realistic, not what would be actually heard "on the street," Williams's artistic achievement is all the more remarkable. Only in later years has this been appreciated; earlier his dialogue was judged "arty" by those whose ears and sensibilities were attuned only to street realism on the stage.

It is evident from Williams's production notes and directions that the music, "romantic" lighting, and background noises of animals, birds, women, children, and railroad are an accompaniment to a paean of love in which "snatching the eternal out of the desperately fleeting is the great magic trick of human existence." The quote is from one of Williams's best articles on theater, "The Timeless World of a Play," the Sunday piece he wrote for the *New York Times* before the opening of *The Rose Tattoo,* now printed as the foreword in some editions of the text.

Here he points out that drama gives us "a world *outside* of time. . . . In a play, time is arrested in the sense of being confined. By a sort of legerdemain, events are made to remain *events,* rather than being reduced so quickly to mere *occurrences.*" In the theater, where the characters are "immured against the corrupting rush of time," we are able to appreciate their humanity, as we do not "have to compete with their virtues nor resist their offenses." Thus, "our hearts are wrung by recognition and pity." Yet George Jean Nathan, a constant Williams detractor, who rewrote some of the dialogue of *The Glass Menagerie,* pronounced this article a "pseudo-learned treatise," which "seeks to justify his alley-cat stuff and indeed make it a cosmic epic." [9]

In his article in *Vogue* magazine in 1951 Williams says that the "Dionysian element in human life" in *The Rose Tattoo* includes "the lyric as well as the Bacchantic impulse . . . [and] it must not be confused with mere sexuality. It is higher and more distilled than that. . . . It is the desire of an artist to work in new forms, however awkwardly at first, to break down barriers of what he has done before and what others have done better before and after." [10]

In its Broadway production, which opened 3 February 1951, it was difficult to perceive Williams's higher aims, but the play pleased audiences and ran for 306 performances. The reviews were mixed but generally favorable. John Mason Brown observed, "Not since the Houses of York and Lancaster feuded long and publicly have roses been used more lavishly. . . . to Mr. Williams roses are mystical signs, proofs of passion, symbols of devotion, and buds no less than thorns in the flesh." [11]

Maureen Stapleton was Serafina, Eli Wallach Alvaro, and Daniel Mann directed, with setting by Boris Aronson. It was no secret that, for the role of Serafina, Williams had in mind Anna Magnani, the great Italian film star. Her larger-than-life, neorealistic approach to acting might have conveyed the play's extra dimensions; its richer values, depths of perception and characterization, symbolism, nuances, and overall style and spirit were missing from this presentation. Its critical and commercial success was due to the artistry of Williams's writing, which has survived many mediocre productions.

The 1955 film version was fortunate in that it secured Anna Magnani for the role of Serafina but unfortunate in that Daniel Mann again directed, so that the values just mentioned were again missing and the problem compounded by a literal, spell-it-all-out script. This being the

1950s, there is no liaison between Serafina and Alvaro and, therefore, no pregnancy, the triumph of life over death with which the play ends. Instead, Alvaro arrives drunk for the assignation and collapses on the floor, in which state it is assumed he spends the night.

In June 1991 Peter Hall directed a noteworthy revival in London, starring Julie Walters as Serafina. It was praised by Michael Billington in the *Guardian* of 13 June as "an attack on social pretense and a hymn to fertility. . . . a robust and life-enhancing comedy in praise of sex." The joyous production forty years after its premiere was testimony to the play's enduring, universal appeal.

Notes

1. Tennessee Williams, "The Meaning of *The Rose Tattoo*," *Vogue,* March 1951, 96.

2. Tennessee Williams, "Author's Note," in *The Theatre of Tennessee Williams* (New York: New Directions, 1971–1992), 7:56.

3. Williams, "Meaning of *The Rose Tattoo*," 96.

4. John L. Styan, "On Tears and Laughter: *The Rose Tattoo,*" *The Dark Comedy: The Development of Modern Comic Tragedy* (Cambridge: Cambridge University Press, 1968), 49–51.

5. Gerald Weales, *Tennessee Williams* (Minneapolis: University of Minnesota Press, 1965), 9.

6. Signi L. Falk, *Tennessee Williams* (New York: Twayne Publishers, 1961), 102, 97.

7. Williams, "Meaning of *The Rose Tattoo*," 96.

8. Williams echoes Eliot's "a handful of dust," in *The Waste Land*, l. 30. Eliot's influence is discussed more fully in chapter 6.

9. George Jean Nathan,"The Rose Tattoo," *The Theatre Book of the Year, 1950–1951* (New York: Alfred A. Knopf, 1951), 210.

10. Williams, "Meaning of *The Rose Tattoo*," 96.

11. John Mason Brown, "Saying It With Flowers," *Saturday Review of Literature* 34 (10 March 1951): 23–24.

CHAPTER SIX

Camino Real

Camino Real is a dream play, described by Don Quixote in the prologue as "a pageant, a masque in which old meanings will be remembered and possibly new ones discovered." Like a dream, it is filled with symbols, inhabited by strangers and well-known personalities, located in an unknown terrain outside of time, and haunted by fear and uncertainty through which hope glimmers. The arrival and departure of Don Quixote frames the action. He enters with Sancho Panza down the central aisle of the auditorium and proceeds to the stage, as Sancho reads a map describing the locale: "the square of a walled town which is the end of the *Ca*mino Re*al* and the beginning of the *Ca*mino Re*al*. Halt there . . . and turn back, Traveler, for the spring of humanity has gone dry in this place."

The central event is a visit by Kilroy, an all-American soldier resembling those in World War II who inscribed "Kilroy Was Here" on venues around the world. On the Camino Real events unfold and characters drift in and out as they would in a dream, without transition or explanation. Being a dream, the play has significance beyond its literal action. Its symbols, says Williams, are drawn from the "great vocabulary of images" in our "conscious and unconscious minds." In an article written before the Broadway opening for the 15 March 1953 Sunday *New York Times,* he explains that the play is "my conception of the time and world that I live in, and its people are mostly archetypes of certain basic attitudes and qualities.... A convention of the play is existence outside of time in a place of no specific locality. If you regard it that way, I suppose it becomes an elaborate allegory."

In his allegory of "the time and world I live in," Williams's Camino Real, a microcosm of the world, is inhabited by a society that includes the richest, Lord and Lady Mulligan, and the poorest, A. Bum. In depicting this society, Williams employs a favorite technique, that of dramatic contrasts. In opposition to the fictional and historical romantic figures of Marguerite Gautier (Camille), Jacques Casanova, and Lord Byron are the hard-hearted, powerful authorities, Gutman and his soldiers, the Street Cleaners, and the medical team. Orderly and efficient, they represent repression, exploitation, and destruction. In between are those out for the main chance, the "Yankee Dollar," like the Gypsy, her son, and the Loan Shark. The Street People, given to dance, song, prostitution, and petty thievery, are a disheveled and disorderly lot, kept distracted by fiestas and checked by strong-armed henchmen of Gutman, who reports to an absent "Generalissimo." Gutman serves as interlocutor and presenter who runs the show on the Camino Real. He announces the "blocks" and the events to come and, at the end, rings down the final curtain.

The themes of this work are constant in Williams's plays: desire versus death, Time as destroyer, the exploitation of the weak and romantic by the tough and realistic, the fear of "time [and] mortality and a failure of love to neutralize either of these forces," to use Williams's words. Another theme will reach its fullest expression in *The Night of the Iguana*—the "humble nobility" of concern for another human being rather than for oneself, as Casanova displays for Marguerite.

The title itself is symbolic. Anglicized, with the accent on the first syllable, it means "real road," the locale of the action. But pronounced with a Spanish inflection, accented on the second syllable of each word, it means "royal road," the past of those who were once the royalty of fact and fable. As Sancho Panza points out, the royal road (of the past) ends at the real road, the present.

In an "unspecified Latin-American country" Williams brings together a group of tourists from past and present, history and fiction. In transit through *Ca*mino *Re*al the great romantics of the "royal" past meet the local inhabitants, who try to prevent their escape—tough authorities, manipulators, and con artists. On the *Ca*mino *Re*al Williams's glorious Romantic-era personages are now figures of fun, ridiculed by the cynical inhabitants, pushed around by petty authority, gypped by the Gypsy, robbed by the people of the "real" street. Time has rendered Casanova and Marguerite impotent, Byron is written out, and Don Quixote is so disreputable that even Sancho Panza deserts him. Yet they are not defeated. Casanova and Marguerite at least have companionship, though she continually betrays him. Byron

CAMINO REAL

goes off to fight for Greece, and Don Quixote departs through the feared "Terra Incognita" (in Williams's words, "a wasteland") to new adventures, taking Kilroy with him.

While the play is "outside of time," the narrative of Kilroy's visit is chronological; he arrives, interacts with the inhabitants, and departs. As a former boxer, he is accustomed to contests, to playing the game with rules that are defined and time that is regulated. But now he has a count against him, an enlarged heart that restrains him from boxing and from sexual relations with his wife. At the end he sums up his visit as "stewed, screwed and tattooed on the Camino Real!" He has survived humiliation, two chases, robbery, a fertility ritual in which he is the "chosen hero," and even death itself, followed by resurrection. Within that framework, as in dreams and in the stream-of-consciousness technique in poetry and novel, characters appear and vanish, with no transition and little exposition. Dance, music, and movement are integral to the action.

Benjamin Nelson complains that the characters represent "attitudes rather than individuals and thus their plights become abstractions." [1] His complaint is representative of those who insisted on realism when the play was produced. To develop the group as individuals rather than as "archetypes," as Williams intends, is hardly consistent with a dream play.

A convention of dreams is the attempted escape from a threatening situation, a recurring Williams theme. In Block Nine a nonscheduled plane, the Fugitivo, arrives, from which passengers disembark, while the tourists from the hotel scramble to board. They include a desperate Marguerite, but she has no reservation or papers. Though Jacques frantically tries to secure them in time, she is refused passage. Later news arrives of the crash of the Fugitivo.

Hovering on the fringes of the plaza are the menacing Street Cleaners, figures of death. The only places of residence are, of course, hotels; on one side of the street, controlled by Gutman, is the exclusive Siete Mares, and on the other the Ritz Men Only, a "flea-bag hotel or flophouse."

Williams describes the play as "poetic" and its symbols and "dream-like images" as "the natural speech of drama": "We all have in our conscious and unconscious minds a great vocabulary of images, and I think all human communication is based on these images as are our dreams; and a symbol in a play has only one legitimate purpose which is to say a thing more directly and simply and beautifully than it could be said in words," he states in the *Times* article.

The use of symbolism, the stream of consciousness, the theme of desire, death, and resurrection, of destruction of cities, of sterility and life-giving water, the allusions, and even the choice of characters and settings reveal the influence of T. S. Eliot, the reigning poet of Williams's day. In 1944 Williams prefaced his early poetry with an acknowledgment of Eliot, Hart Crane, and Rilke as influences upon his writing.[2] Crane was yet to achieve his later prominence, but on campuses all over the country in the years Williams was in college (1929–1930,1936–1938), "The Love Song of J. Alfred Prufrock" and *The Waste Land* were the most read, discussed, attacked, and defended of all modern poetry.

Eliot's dictum that everyday speech, not poetic diction, should be the basis of modern poetry is brilliantly displayed in *The Waste Land,* a poem that includes whole scenes of dialogue. One of Williams's most important contributions to American drama is his poetic dialogue, which, notes Arthur Miller, "lifted lyricism to its highest level in our theater's history."[3] Although echoes of Eliot can be heard in many of Williams's plays, his use of heightened colloquialism to create the cadences and diction of poetry are especially evident in *Camino Real.* The choice of Marguerite, Casanova, and Byron as characters reflects Eliot's contrast of the heroic past with the ineffectual present, in such poems as "The Love Song of J. Alfred Prufrock" and "Sweeney among the Nightingales."

"Prufrock" and *The Waste Land* may provide a key for better understanding *Camino Real.* Williams's Gypsy is a down-to-earth Madame Sosostris, whose cards, as in *The Waste Land,* reveal past, present, and future.[4] A. Bum in *Camino,* who leans out of the window of a fleabag hotel, is reminiscent of the lonely men who lean out of windows in "Prufrock,"[5] in which there are cheap, one-night hotels. A.

Bum, who sings snatches of old popular songs, has one word of dialogue: "Lonely." Eliot's *Waste Land* images of sterility and parched earth relieved by rain in "What the Thunder Said" become Williams's actual fountain in the square, dry until Don Quixote at the end restores it, symbolically reviving "the spring of humanity," which had gone dry.

The sterility of the couples in "A Game of Chess" in *The Waste Land* is reflected in the sterility of the relationship between Casanova and Marguerite. Gutman's cry in Block Seven—"it's like the fall of a capital city, the destruction of Carthage, the sack of Rome by the white-eyed giants from the North! I've seen them fall! I've seen the destruction of them!"—echoes Eliot's destruction of the cities in "What the Thunder Said."[6]

Like modern poetry and like dreams, *Camino Real* dispenses with transitions, its incidents moving from Block to Block, announced by Gutman not in time, like a realistic play, but outside of time. Although Casanova and Marguerite attempt to escape from the present into the future, they are as they are because of their past on the Royal Road, which has led them to the present Real Road, from which they cannot escape any more than they can escape from the past. Unlike their fictional representation as archetypical romantic lovers, on the *Camino Real* they are weak and aging. Byron confesses that he is written out and departs for Greece.

CAMINO REAL

into parting with all his money. Despite the setbacks, Kilroy remains buoyant and good-humored, even though his man-in-the-street views are challenged at every turn on the Camino Real. He meets the Baron on Block Four:

> KILROY: Hey, mate. It's wonderful to see you. . . . A normal American. In a clean white suit.
> THE BARON: My suit is pale yellow. My nationality is French, and my normality has been often subject to question.

This being a fantasy, a happy ending is possible; in Block Sixteen the resurrected Kilroy leaves Camino Real for Terra Incognita with Don Quixote, as the Don exclaims, *"The violets in the mountains have broken the rocks!"*

Williams's dramatic use of dichotomy in characterization and in the themes of death and desire, time past and time present, and the royal road and the real road, can be seen as well in the expressions of idealism and cynicism, hope and despair. In Block Ten Marguerite voices the uncertainty of the existential world of *Camino Real,* which Williams sees as a microcosm of the "world that I live in": "What are we sure of? Not even of our existence. . . . and whom can we ask the questions that torment us? 'What is this place?' 'Where are we?' . . . Where? Why? and the perch that we hold is unstable! We're threatened with eviction, for this is a port of entry and departure, there are no permanent guests! And where else have we to go when we leave here? . . . tenderness, the violets in the mountains—can't break the rocks!" But Jacques replies, "The violets in the mountains can break the rocks if you believe in them and allow them to grow!"

The play abounds in allusions and images that enrich the panoply of life as seen by Williams, part circus celebration, part deadly and threatening, but never without gallantry in the face of despair, even on the part of the smallest and weakest. Gutman may observe of the sunset, "These are the moments when we look into ourselves and ask with a wonder which never is lost altogether: 'Can this be all? Is there nothing more? Is this what the glittering wheels of the heavens turn for?'" He may see the inhabitants of Camino Real as "thieves and petty vendors in a bazaar where the human heart is part of the bargain." But Esmeralda will pray for all the inhabitants in Block Sixteen: "all con men and hustlers and pitch-men who hawk their hearts on the street, all two-time losers who're likely to lose once more." Familiar Williams images include life-giving water that springs from the once dried fountain, as a symbol of hope, and birds as symbols of the soul. In Camino Real all birds are caged, but when Byron leaves he takes them along. Kilroy's enlarged heart not only is a physical threat but also symbolizes two well-worn adages (to use his own idiom) about his character, that he is "big-hearted" and has a "heart of gold."

Colors are employed symbolically, with Esmeralda in green, as a fertility goddess, the Madrecita in black, and the Baron in yellow. In Kilroy's encounter with the perennial virgin Esmeralda, removing her veil symbolizes intercourse, followed in Block Twelve by the common experience of disappointment when expectations fail to meet their promise. The scientists' clinical dissection of Kilroy and the ominous Street Cleaners—a chilling image of Death— represent a cold, inhuman disregard for life, but they are balanced by the caring mother, La Madrecita, who cradles the dead Kilroy like a pietà in Block Fifteen as she delivers a eulogy of praise in contradictory counterpoint to the remarks of the medical instructor.

In Block Eight Byron voices the fear of the artist that his creative powers may be waning: *"There is a passion for declivity in this world!* And lately I've found myself listening to hired musicians behind a row of artificial palm trees—instead of the single—pure-stringed instrument of my heart. . . [Williams's ellipsis] Well, then, it's time to leave here! . . . possibly—the old pure music will come to me again. Of course on the other hand I may hear only the little noise of insects in the grass . . . [Williams's ellipsis] But I am sailing to Athens! *Make voyages!—Attempt them!*—there's nothing else . . ." (Williams's ellipsis). He departs fearlessly up the incline from which others shrink back, shouting "THIS WAY!" to the luggage porters carrying (with a nod to Magritte?) the caged birds. The courage of his departure is marred by the knowledge that he will die in Greece.

There is humor throughout; sometimes it is verbal, as in the incongruity of Kilroy's optimistic clichés in the face of disaster or in the Gypsy's cynical views that fleecing the customer is normal business practice. Her interview of Kilroy parodies such procedures, whether it be for a potential employee or prospective son-in-law. There is physical farce in the chase, in which, in possibly the oldest of farcical situations, a chamber pot is emptied on the head of a complainer. Here the danger to Kilroy is offset by the knowledge that this is "only a dream." Although familiar in modern poetry, the free form, imagery, and dreamlike sequences of *Camino Real* were new to the professional American theater of that day. Williams recalls in *Memoirs* that when he sent the first draft of the play, written in 1946, to his agent, Audrey Wood, she advised him to put the play away and not show it to anyone. Although he longed for a plastic, poetic theater, Williams, after the commercial failure of *Camino Real,* would continue to disguise his poetry through concrete imagery and realistic allusions and would not try a free form again until *Out Cry (The Two-Character Play).* He was ahead of his time.

Audiences and critics found the play tended to "exasperate and confuse" (Williams's words). They were not ready for such a work; neither was the director nor were the actors. *Camino Real* remains today, though virtually unproduced, one of Williams's most challenging, best-written, and most misunderstood works. One of those the play obviously did "exasperate" as well as "confuse" was Signi Falk, who observed that, in developing the play from a shorter version, Williams "added several other romantics, a few sexual perverts, a number of symbolic figures of evil. . . . gave cosmic significance to occasional scenes, and in others, edged toward the pornographic." [9]

During the play's out-of-town tryout Williams reports in his pre-opening Sunday *Times* article of 15 March 1953: "At each performance a number of people have stamped out of the auditorium, with little regard for those whom they have had to crawl over . . . and there have been sibilant noises on the way out and demands for money back. . . . I am at a loss to explain this phenomenon, and if I am being facetious about one thing, I am being quite serious about another when I say that I had never for one minute supposed that the play would seem obscure and confusing to anyone who was willing to meet it even less than half-way."

Four days later *Camino Real* opened at the Martin Beck Theater to a critical reception that was only lukewarm, revealing how thoroughly Williams was misunderstood by most critics: "The genuine element in Tennessee Williams has always seemed to me to be his realism. . . . *Camino* seemed wholly given over to the non-genuine element . . . [and] doesn't even pretend to realism," pronounced Eric Bentley.[10] Brooks Atkinson declared: "There is no health in it. With rare exceptions everyone succumbs to depravity. The Camino Real is a jail-yard of vice." [11] Without "money" reviews the play had a short run of sixty performances and did not recover its substantial investment. During its run a barrage of letters defending the play was published in the *New York Times* as well as an advertisement by supporters calling the play "a work of the imagination . . . romantic, intensely poetic and modern." Among the signers was artist Willem de Kooning, who, unlike the critics, would have had no trouble understanding expressionism.

For the published text Williams "considerably revised" the play, adding a dramatic prologue as well as an explanatory afterword, by way of response to the overcritical and carping reviews. In the afterword, dated 1 June 1953, he replied directly to Eric Bentley, author of *The Playwright as Thinker:* "I have read the works of 'thinking playwrights' as distinguished from us who are permitted only to feel, and probably read them earlier and appreciated them as much as those who invoke their names nowadays like the incantation of Aristophanes's frogs."

Still smarting over the attacks seven years later, Williams defended *Camino Real* in an interview with Arthur Gelb of the *Times* as "a plea for a romantic attitude toward life, which can also be interpreted as a religious attitude—religious in an august, mysterious sense." [12] Harold Clurman commented perceptively on the difficulty of mounting, in the commercial context of Broadway, what was then con-

sidered experimental theater: "The sad fact of our theater is
that a play like *Camino Real* with all its faults ought to be
produced, listened to, criticized with measure and affec-
tion, but that this is difficult when its production costs a
fortune, when it is forced to become part of the grand
machinery of investment, real estate, Broadway brokerage
and competition for reputation." [13]

The play received no help from the production, literal
rather than poetic, earthbound rather than infused with the
"color, the grace and levitation" Williams calls for. In the
afterword he states that "the printed script of a play is hardly
more than an architect's blueprint of a house not yet built":
"The color, the grace and levitation, the structural pattern
in motion, the quick interplay of live beings, suspended like
fitful lightning in a cloud, these things are the play, not
words on paper." It is almost as if he were describing an
ideal production of *Camino,* not what was seen at the
Martin Beck. He concludes, "*Dynamic* is a word in disre-
pute at the moment, and so, I suppose, is the word *organic,*
but those terms still define the dramatic values that I value
most and which I value more as they are more deprecated
by the ones self-appointed to save what they have never
known." The sentence indicates how deeply hurt Williams
was by the reviews of this play.

Judging from the direction by Elia Kazan, the acting,
and the set, one can see why audiences and critics were
confused. A lyric, poetic play was given a realistic produc-

tion. Harold Clurman noted that the production was not only too heavy scenically but "vocally too noisy": "It is too punchy, forthright and 'realistic.' It stampedes where it should float; it clamors and declaims where it should insinuate. It has much less humor than the text." [14]

Years later Kazan would admit in his autobiography that, with the exception of Eli Wallach, the actors were "not up to the needs of their parts. They were trained in a more realistic technique. So was I." [15] The technique he refers to was "the method," the duplication of the real in every detail. Thirty years later David Mamet would attack "the method" as harmful to "the *meaning* of the play." Mamet charges that "actors for the last thirty years have been hiding in a ludicrously incorrect understanding of the Stanislavsky System and employing incorrectly understood jargon as an excuse for not acting. . . . To have this never-ceasing concern with one's [the actor's] personal comfort, with the 'naturalness' of the script . . . is to reduce every play to the *same* play." [16]

Three years later, in 1956, the NET Playhouse presented on public television a much more effective production, using the original, shorter series of scenes, *Ten Blocks on the Camino Real,* which Williams had written in 1946. The Broadway play was a revision, expanding the blocks to sixteen.

By 1970, when the play was revived at the Vivian Beaumont Theater with Al Pacino as Kilroy, it no longer seemed obscure. As Clive Barnes commented in his review in the *New York Times* of 9 January, "our standards of obscurity, like our standards of obscenity, have escalated since those dark days of theatrical innocence." Barnes saw the play "as a symbolic portrait of the American poet . . . of genius lavishly misspent, a defiant play about defeat, a play with the shabby smell of death to it . . . a lovely play, a play of genuinely poetic vision. . . . Seen now from the brink of the 'seventies, *Camino Real* seems oddly prophetic about its author." [17]

Notes

1. Benjamin Nelson, *Tennessee Williams: The Man and His Work* (New York: Ivan Obolensky, 1961), 183.

2. Tennessee Williams, "Preface to My Poems," in *Five Young American Poets* (Norfolk, Conn.: New Directions, 1944), 124–26.

3. Arthur Miller, "Tennessee Williams's Legacy," *TV Guide,* 3 March 1984, 30.

4. T. S. Eliot, *The Waste Land,* l. 46.

5. Eliot, "The Love Song of J. Alfred Prufrock," ll. 6, 72.

6. Eliot, *The Waste Land,* ll. 373–76.

7. Ibid., ll. 177–79.

8. Harold Bloom, "Introduction," in *Tennessee Williams: Modern Critical Views,* ed. Harold Bloom (New York: Chelsea House, 1987), 2.

9. Signi L. Falk, *Tennessee Williams* (New York: Twayne Publishers, 1961), 120.

10. Eric Bentley, "Camino Real," *New Republic* 128, 30 March 1953, 30–31.

11. Brooks Atkinson, "Theater," *New York Times,* 20 March 1953, 26.

12. Arthur Gelb, "Williams and Kazan and the Big Walk-Out," *New York Times,* 1 May 1960, 2:1, 3.

13. Harold Clurman, "Tennessee Williams," *The Divine Pastime: Theatre Essays* (New York: Macmillan, 1974), 23.

14. Ibid.

15. Elia Kazan, *A Life* (New York: Alfred A. Knopf, 1988), 498.

16. David Mamet, "Realism," *Writing in Restaurants* (New York: Viking Penguin, 1986), 132–33.

17. Clive Barnes, "Theater," *New York Times,* 9 January 1970, 42.

CHAPTER SEVEN

Cat on a Hot Tin Roof

Cat on a Hot Tin Roof is a near classical tragedy, in which a larger-than-life "king" of his domain, Big Daddy, with his son Brick relentlessly pursues the truth, despite the mendacity and deception that hide it. Both of them gain stature by the pursuit but lose the fight against death and the race against time. The resolution, as Williams states, is ambiguous, not "pat." But there also is the promise of a new life. Like classical drama, the play focuses not only upon individuals but upon a group.

The crisis the Pollits face is one common to all families, the death of its head: "I'm trying to catch the true quality of experience in a group of people, that cloudy, flickering, evanescent—fiercely charged!—interplay of live human beings in the thundercloud of a common crisis," says Williams in a comment on Brick in act 2. The crisis cannot be resolved because there is no communication, only misunderstanding and mistrust, between the members of the family. "Nobody sees anybody truly but all through the flaws of their own egos," Williams wrote Elia Kazan early in their working relationship. "Vanity, fear, desire, competition—all such distortions within our own egos—condition our vision of those in relation to us. Add to those distortions in our *own* egos, the corresponding distortions in the egos of *others,* and you see how cloudy the glass must become through which we look at each other." [1]

When asked about influences on his plays Williams often mentioned Chekhov. In this, the most Chekhovian of his plays, both individual and group are significant, yet in their relationships they fail to communicate, for each character's vision of another is seen through a cloudy glass, distorted by his or her own ego.

From his 1952 short story "Three Players of a Summer Game" Williams takes the names of Brick and Maggie (Margaret). A former athlete, Brick is an alcoholic, no reason being given other than "there must have been something else that he wanted and lacked." [2] Margaret is an unsympathetic character who resembles Strindberg's women. When Brick succumbs to drink, she withholds sex as part of her strategy to gain emotional and financial dominance over him. Other than a transition from soft to tough, she bears little resemblance to Maggie "the Cat" of the drama, of whom Williams says in his "Note of Explanation": "It so happened that Maggie the Cat had become steadily more charming to me as I worked on her characterization." Other carryovers from his story, which takes place in the course of a summer, are the croquet games and winning and losing as symbolism. The story hints of an affinity between Brick and a young doctor who dies and whose wife becomes Brick's mistress, during which interlude he regains stability, only to lose it again. The atmosphere is that of realism on the edge of fantasy.

CAT ON A HOT TIN ROOF

In the drama, in her first-act monologue in their bed-sitting-room at Big Daddy's plantation, the more appealing Maggie, desperate to preserve a precarious marriage, compares herself to a cat on a hot tin roof: "My hat is still in the ring, and I am determined to win!—What is the victory of a cat on a hot tin roof?—I wish I knew. . . . Just staying on it, I guess, as long as she can. . . ." (ellipses both Williams's). Knowing that Big Daddy, dying of cancer, has not yet made a will and that Brick is his favorite son, she is intent on gaining the inheritance for herself and Brick. But Brick, devoting himself to drink, refuses to resist the efforts of his grasping brother Gooper and sister-in-law Mae to be named the heirs. Maggie's determination to inherit is as strong as her yearning for Brick to resume their physical relationship, which Brick has broken off. She knows that the struggle has changed her: "I've gone through this—*hideous!—transformation,* become—*hard! Frantic!* . . . —*cruel!!*

Maggie's background, her relationship with Brick, her concern for Big Daddy, and her antagonism toward Gooper and Mae—all are revealed to Brick, who, in Chekhovian fashion, seems not to hear her, as he is preoccupied with private thought. He has broken his ankle the night before and is on crutches; his only movement is to replenish his drink, as she chatters: "Mae an' Gooper are plannin' to freeze us out of Big Daddy's estate because you drink and I'm childless. But we can defeat that plan. We're *going* to defeat that plan! *Brick, y'know, I've been so God damn disgustingly poor all my life!"* Part of Mae and Gooper's advantage is that they have five children, and, although Maggie knows that having a child with Brick would insure their inheritance, he is uncooperative.

The one-sided conversation mounts to a climax with the mention of Brick's dead friend, Skipper. According to the facts brought out by Maggie in this act, Skipper had a secret, homosexual love for Brick, of which Maggie was aware, but Brick was not. In Brick's absence she had confronted Skipper with this fact, and Skipper had tried, but failed, to prove his manhood by attempting to have sex with Maggie. Although Brick had learned of the incident from both Maggie and Skipper, he blames Maggie for Skipper's death from drink. The act concludes with Maggie telling Brick, "This is my time by the calendar to conceive."

> BRICK: . . . how in hell on earth do you imagine—that you're going to have a child by a man that can't stand you?
> MARGARET: That's a problem that I will have to work out.

Williams observes the classical unities of place, time, and action in this play. In its single setting, the "fair summer sky . . . fades into dusk and night during the course of the play, which occupies precisely the time of its performance," states Williams's "Notes for the Designer." In act

CAT ON A HOT TIN ROOF

1 Maggie is the center of attention, as she circles, entices, preens, confesses, and pleads. In contrast, virtually the entire cast is onstage in act 2. Because Brick is on crutches, Big Daddy's birthday party (his last, unknown to him) will be held in Brick's room. The injury to Brick, which Williams makes so convincing, is also a theatrical device to confine all of the action to a single setting.

This play marks an advance over Williams's previous works in that three, not one or two, major characters are developed, giving rise to double conflicts, one between Maggie and Brick and the other between Brick and Big Daddy. Williams uses the classical duologue to develop these conflicts in the opening scene between Maggie and Brick and at the end of act 2, between Brick and his father. He employs monologue at the opening, and a "chorus" of children, orchestrated by Mae, their mother and leader.

Big Daddy is the "star" of act 2. As was true with Maggie, his dialogue reveals his history as well as his character. He is big in stature, emotions, possessions. He left school at ten, worked in the fields, became a tramp who hopped off a freight car "half a mile down the road," and became overseer of the land owned by Jack Straw and Peter Ochello, homosexuals who later died. Big Daddy then took over the land and developed it into "twenty-eight thousand acres of the richest land this side of the valley Nile."

The scene between Brick and Big Daddy hit home to so many in the audience who had undergone the same failure to communicate with children on serious matters that they emerged visibly shaken at intermission. (Miller's *Death of a Salesman* had a similar effect.) By the time the two have their talk it is known that Brick's drinking is related to his friend Skipper—more will come out—and to Brick's having failed as an athlete: "Time just outran me, Big Daddy—got there first."

Big Daddy and Brick have talked before: "But this talk is like all the others we've ever had together in our lives! It's nowhere, nowhere!—it's—it's *painful,* Big Daddy. . . ." (Williams's ellipsis). But Big Daddy persists. He wants both to root out the reason for Brick's alcoholism and to confide in a loved one his relief that he is not dying of cancer. (The medical report, which was positive, has been withheld from Big Daddy and his wife, who have been told the opposite.) "Yep. I thought I had it. The earth shook under my foot, the sky come down . . . and I couldn't breathe!—Today!! I drew my first free breath in—how many years?—*God!—three.* . . ." (Williams's ellipsis).

He persists in asking why Brick drinks, even to taking away his crutch and withholding his liquor. Brick says it is "disgust" with "mendacity"—"lying and liars." Big Daddy replies that he has put up with lying and liars and pretenses all his life (with dramatic irony, he has accepted the biggest lie of all, that he is free of cancer): "You and being a success as a planter is all I ever had any devotion to in my whole life! . . . *I've* lived with mendacity!—Why can't *you* live with it?

CAT ON A HOT TIN ROOF

Hell, you *got* to live with it." Brick indicates that he doesn't care whether or not he inherits the plantation and tries to leave.

> BIG DADDY: "Don't let's—leave it like this, like them other talks we've had . . . it's always like something was left not spoken. . . .
> BRICK: But we've never *talked* to each other.
> BIG DADDY: We can *now*. . . . you're passin' the buck to things like time and disgust with 'mendacity' . . . and I'm not buying any. . . . You started drinkin' when your friend Skipper died.

Driven beyond his emotional reserve, Brick decides that all the truth will be told, including the truth about Big Daddy's dying of cancer. He reveals that Maggie put in Skipper's mind "the dirty, false idea that what we were, him and me, was a frustrated case of that ole pair of sisters that lived in this room. . . . He, poor Skipper, went to bed with Maggie to prove it wasn't true, and when it didn't work out, he thought it *was* true! . . . nobody ever turned so fast to a lush—or died of it so quick . . ."

> BIG DADDY: Something's left out of that story. . . .
> BRICK: Yes!—I left out a long-distance call which I had from Skipper, in which he made a drunken confession to me and on which I hung up!—last time

we spoke to each other in our lives. . . . [Williams's ellipsis]

BIG DADDY: . . . This disgust with mendacity is disgust with yourself. *You!*—dug the grave of your friend and kicked him in it!—before you'd face the truth with him!

BRICK: *His* truth, not *mine!*

Then Brick reveals the truth to Big Daddy: "Who *can* face truth? Can *you*? . . . . *How about these birthday congratulations, these many, many happy returns of the day, when ev'rybody but you knows there won't be any!*" He then retreats—"I said what I said without thinking." Big Daddy rushes from the room.

In the play as originally written and in Howard Davies's 1990 Broadway revival Big Daddy does not appear again. Just before the end, during the final dialogue between Maggie and Brick, from offstage "a long drawn cry of agony and rage fills the house. . . . The cry is repeated." Both the offstage cry and its powerful effect on the audience are reminiscent of classical tragedy.

As if to demonstrate the truth of Brick's charge of mendacity, the third act begins with the family plus the doctor and minister hovering about Big Mama, telling her the painful truth about Big Daddy and urging her to sign legal documents giving Gooper and Mae the inheritance. While they are pressuring Big Mama and insinuating about

Brick's drinking and irresponsibility, Maggie attacks: "I've never seen such malice toward a brother. . . . This is a deliberate campaign of vilification for the most disgusting and sordid reason on earth, and I know what it is! It's *avarice, avarice, greed, greed!*"

The play not only adheres to the classical unities, but it also follows the pattern of a well-made play, with exposition in the first act, climax in the second, and resolution in the third. Told the truth in clinical, realistic detail by Gooper, Big Mama replies with acceptance: "Time goes by so fast. Nothin' can outrun it. Death commences too early—almost before you're half-acquainted with life—you meet with the other. . . ." (Williams's ellipsis).

She turns to Brick and embraces him: "Oh, Brick, son of Big Daddy! Big Daddy does so love you! Y'know what would be his fondest dream come true? If before he passed on, if Big Daddy has to pass on, you gave him a child of yours, a grandson as much like his son as his son is like Big Daddy!" Maggie's "announcement" follows: "Brick and I are going to—*have a child!*" Monosyllabic, iambic, the single sentence in ten seconds brings dramatic impact and surprise to the scene and promises a resolution.

In the play's closing moments, with Maggie and Brick left onstage, she tells him that she will achieve her aim of becoming pregnant "by locking his liquor up and making him satisfy my desire before I unlock it!" The "groaning cry" of Big Daddy is heard offstage again, and, in answer to the herald of death, Maggie, who has informed Brick earlier that it is her "time by the calendar to conceive," now tells him, "And so tonight we're going to make the lie true. . . ." As the curtain begins to fall, she asserts, "I *do* love you, Brick, I *do!*" and the play ends, quietly, magically, as Brick's final line echoes Big Daddy's ironic doubt of a simple declaration of love, "Wouldn't it be funny if that was true?"

In the conflicts between Maggie and Brick and Big Daddy and Brick the complex characters of all three are revealed. Maggie and Big Daddy share a fighting spirit, and Big Mama says that Brick "is like Big Daddy." Both Maggie and Big Daddy have had to struggle upward from poor beginnings, which helps to explain their material and emotional possessiveness. Brick's weakness they counter with strength and resourceful determination to hold onto what they love. While Maggie sees herself as a cat, Big Daddy likens himself to a fist: "All of my life I been like a doubled up fist. . . .—Poundin', smashin', drivin'!" (Williams's ellipsis). Both are tolerant: "One thing you can grow on a big place more important than cotton!—is *tolerance!*—I grown it," says Big Daddy. Maggie genuinely cares for Big Daddy and Big Mama, as they for her.

Brick, in contrast to them, has never had to struggle: he has grown up rich, pampered, good-looking, and loved, his parents' favorite. He has never had to face the hard knocks that might have matured him. He and Maggie had enjoyed a happy physical relationship earlier in their marriage; she says he was a "wonderful" lover, and when Big Daddy asks, "How was Maggie in bed?" Brick replies, "Great! the greatest!" His nickname may come from his red hair (Big Mama recalls him as a little boy, "his—red curls shining") but, as the names of Williams's characters often carry symbolic significance, it may also ironically suggest the strength Brick lacks. He is unprepared to face the reality that will face Chance Wayne in *Sweet Bird of Youth,* that, for those who have only good looks and/or athletic ability, youth is fleeting and time, as Brick realizes, cannot be outrun; Brick has learned this the night before the play's action begins, when, drunk, he attempted to jump hurdles on the athletic field and broke his ankle.

The picture of him at curtain rise, then, is of a handsome, damaged athlete on crutches, a drink in his hand. He drinks to escape a truth he cannot face, that he caused his friend Skipper's death. He drinks until he hears a "click" in his head which brings him peace; possibly the sound is that of the phone when he hung up on Skipper's "drunken confession" of love. But, as Brick tells his father, that was "*his* truth, not *mine!*"

Thus, there is nothing in the reports of the past or in Brick's behavior in the play to suggest that he is a homosexual, nor was he so played by the actor here mentioned. As Maggie points out in act 1, handsome sports figures are attractive to both sexes. But some critics resented the ambiguity. In his *New York Herald Tribune* review of 25 March 1955 Walter Kerr charged that "there is . . . a tantalizing reluctance . . . to let the play blurt out its promised secret": "This isn't due to the nerve-wracking, extraordinarily prolonged silence of its central figure. . . . It is due to the fact that when we come to a fiery scene of open confession—between a belligerent father and his defiant son—the truth still dodges around verbal corners, slips somewhere between the veranda shutters, refuses to meet us on firm, clear terms."

In the stage directions for the father-son scene in act 2 of the reading version of the play, Williams replied to charges that the characterization of Brick was not clear-cut enough: "The bird that I hope to catch in the net of this play is not the solution of one man's psychological problem. . . . Some mystery should be left in the revelation of character in a play. . . . This does not absolve the playwright of his duty to observe and probe as clearly and deeply as he legitimately can: but it should steer him away from 'pat' conclusions, facile definitions which make a play just a play, not a snare for the truth of human experience."

In his reply to Kerr, in an article titled "Critic Says 'Evasion,' Writer Says 'Mystery'" Williams explains:

> You may prefer to be told precisely what to believe about every character in a play. . . . Then I am not your playwright. My characters make my play. I always start with them, they take spirit and body in my

mind. Nothing that they say or do is arbitrary or invented. They build the play about them. . . . I live with them for a year and a half or two years and I know them far better than I know myself. . . . But still they must have that quality of life which is shadowy. . . . Brick's overt sexual adjustment was, and must always remain, a heterosexual one. He will go back to Maggie for sheer animal comfort.[3]

Esther Jackson is quite clear in her conviction that Brick is a homosexual and "guilty of a crime, a transgression so dreadful that neither he nor his family dare speak its name": "Williams finds in homosexuality an equivalent for the Greek sin of incest."[4] Arthur Ganz, examining Williams as a moralist, points out that Brick is punished for his rejection of Skipper, just as Blanche was for rejecting her husband, Allan.[5] Signi Falk links Big Daddy's remark "It's always like something [in earlier talks] was left not spoken" to Williams's one-act *Something Unspoken,* in which he "plays with the idea of lesbianism . . . [and] again the handling of the topic is evasive, deliberately so."[6]

On 28 March 1955, four days after the opening, Williams was the guest at the luncheon meeting of the Drama Desk, a New York organization of theater editors and critics. When asked about Brick's characterization he replied, "I think there should always be an element of the unresolved in the theater—an element of the incompletely answered—we should go out of the theater still wondering, as we go out of life. . . . I'm not able to give pat conclusions . . . I don't believe pat conclusions are true."[7] In an interview with *Theatre Arts* magazine Williams said that Brick was not a homosexual, that his self-disgust was the result of living so long with lies.[8]

It is now possible to view Brick's character in the context of the play as a whole and to see that the question of homosexuality is not the issue. The symbolism of games and game playing, of winning and losing, provides a clue to Brick's disillusionment with the world. For a young, handsome athlete the world of games is an ideal one. As Johan Huizinga points out, in "play" there are "certain limits of time and space" as well as "a visible order," and rules are "freely accepted, and outside the sphere of necessity or material utility."[9]

But, as Brick learns, life outside the playing field is neither so orderly nor so simple. His ideal marriage and his ideal friendship are both destroyed when Skipper breaks the rules with his drunken confession, to which Brick reacts not with understanding but with disgust, ending the phone conversation and the friendship. The once glorious athlete is now on crutches. Hamlet-like, Brick now sees only lies, betrayal, sickness, and mendacity in a world that once cheered his heroism.

Arthur Miller views Brick as "a lonely young man sensitized to injustice. Around him is a world . . . of grossness, Philistinism, greed, money-lust, power-lust. . . . In contrast, Brick conceives of his friendship with his dead

CAT ON A HOT TIN ROOF

friend as an idealistic . . . relationship . . . beyond the realm of price, of value, even of materiality. He clings to this image as to a banner of purity to flaunt against the world, and more precisely, against the decree of nature to reproduce himself, to become in turn the father, the master of the earth, the administrator of the tainted and impure world." [10]

Of the minor characters Mae, Gooper, and their five "no-neck" children have few redeeming traits. The couple are at the birthday party to see that Big Mama signs the papers lawyer Gooper has drawn up, so that the estate will become theirs. There is some sympathy for Gooper when he confesses in act 3, "I've resented Big Daddy's partiality to Brick ever since Brick was born, and the way I've been treated like I was just barely good enough to spit on and sometimes not even good enough for that." Together with the doctor, who has lied to Big Daddy and Big Mama about the medical report, and the preacher, "sincere as a bird-call blown on a hunter's whistle," Mae and Gooper personify the mendacity that disgusts Brick.

Of Big Mama Williams says that "she is very sincere." All the characters except Big Mama have egos that impede their understanding of others. She is the only unselfish, loving family member. She is aware that Big Daddy's jokes at her expense are expressions of his disappointment with their marriage. Her own jokes are a cover for her hurt. Her sincerity and goodness contrast with the mendacity of the quartet. When told the truth in act 3 about Big Daddy's condition, she refuses to accept it, insisting, "It's just a bad dream." The wrangling over the estate, Gooper's threat to sue for his share, and his thrusting of legal papers at her evoke an outburst from Big Mama: "I'm talkin' in Big Daddy's language now; I'm his *wife,* not his *widow,* I'm still his *wife!* . . . I say CRAP too, like Big Daddy! . . . *Nobody's goin' to take nothin'!*—till Big Daddy lets go of it."

Each of the principal characters has his or her individual idiom, with rhythms and imagery that flavor the dialogue and deepen the characterization. Big Daddy's speeches are monosyllabic, their allusions are to commonplace objects, and behind all of them lurk the pitiless figures of Time and Death. He is materialistic, in the vain hope that what is substantial can bring the comfort of permanence and relieve the terror that haunts him. He confides to Brick in act 2:

> That Europe is nothin' on earth but a great big auction . . . it's just a big fire-sale . . . an' Big Mama wint wild in it. . . . Bought, bought, bought! . . . It's lucky I'm a rich man, it sure is lucky, well, I'm a rich man, Brick, yep, I'm a mighty rich man. . . . But a man can't buy his life with it, he can't buy back his life with it when his life has been spent, that's one thing not offered in the Europe fire-sale or in the American markets or any markets on earth, a man can't buy his life with it, he can't buy back his life when his life is finished. . . .[Williams's ellipsis]

He also views death in terms that link the familiar and the unknown: "I thought I had it . . . the sky come down like the black lid of a kettle and I couldn't breathe!" Characteristic of Big Daddy is his speech on pretense to Brick in the same scene, a speech that combines rhythm, repetition, imagery, and alliteration, culminating with a five-beat spondee: "Think of all the lies I got to put up with!—Pretenses! Ain't that mendacity? . . . Having for instance to act like I care for Big Mama! . . . . Pretend to love that son of a bitch of a Gooper. . . . Church!—it bores the Bejesus out of me. . . . Clubs!—Elks! Masons! Rotary!—*crap!*" One expects coarse allusions and is not disappointed, but these are in character, especially as he fantasizes about taking a mistress. His earthy humor and love of rhyming ("Was it jumping or humping that you were doing out there? What were you doing out there at three A.M., layin' a woman on that cinder track?") turn serious as he leaves at the end of act 2 after hearing the truth about his condition: "All liars, all lying dying liars!—Lying! Dying! Liars!"

Williams states, "I believe that in *Cat* I reached beyond myself, in the second act, to a kind of crude eloquence of expression in Big Daddy that I have managed to give no other character of my creation." [11] Big Daddy's speeches at times are reminiscent of Hart Crane's simple, strong dialogue in his poetry, like the mother's monologue "Indiana," in *The Bridge*. E. Martin Browne notes that Big Daddy "reminds one of a character in Genesis (perhaps from the less frequently quoted chapters). . . . The best poetry of the play is in his speeches, which distil the wisdom of primitive human nature." Browne, who first directed the plays of T. S. Eliot, comments, "Tennessee Williams's use of repetition to create a prison of words is extraordinarily skilful: words beat like a tattoo on the heart, yet the beat is subtly changed at each hearing." [12]

Just as Maggie's movements in act 1 are catlike—preening, stretching, stalking, purring at times, hissing at others—so some of her remarks to Mae are "catty": "But Mae? Why did y'give dawgs' names to all your kiddies?" When asked by Brick why she is "being catty," Maggie replies, "'Cause I'm consumed with envy an' eaten up with longing." Her sentences, such as this one, are often balanced. There is assonance and alliteration in the cadence as well, in keeping with Williams's description of her voice as having "range and music." A significant line may be rhythmic, anapestic: *"I feel all the time like a cat on a hot tin roof!"* Or *"I am Maggie the Cat!"* she remarks to herself in the mirror in act 1. Her allusions in her monologue are to hand-me-down clothes that she has worn and a debut dress "Mother made me from a pattern in *Vogue."* Proper names such as the magazine title occur throughout, grounding the poetry in reality. During her virtual aria Maggie is undressing and dressing, putting on sandals, jewelry, and makeup. Appearance is important to Maggie, because, above all, she wants to remain attractive to Brick: "You know, our sex life didn't just peter out . . . it was cut off short . . . and it's going to revive again. . . . That's what I'm keeping myself attractive for."

Brick is the most complex of the three major characters. He speaks little during Maggie's monologue, barely listening, repeating her last words by way of comment. In their talk together in act 2 he is the same with Big Daddy, until about halfway through the act: "Brick's detachment is at last broken through" read the stage directions. His speeches become longer as he outlines his friendship with Skipper, the conflict between him and Maggie, and the final phone call. Contrary to his earlier, detached repetition of others, he now relays the cruel truth to Big Daddy in short words and direct statements: "We're finally going to have that real true talk you wanted. It's too late to stop it, now, we got to carry it through and cover every subject. . . . Who *can* face truth? Can *you*?" He reveals the truth everyone else had been hiding from Big Daddy—that there will be no more birthday parties or "happy returns of the day."

His apology is softer and slower and more convoluted, as if he were trying hard to think clearly, to explain carefully: "I'm sorry, Big Daddy. My head don't work any more . . . I said what I said without thinking. . . . I don't know but—anyway—we've been friends . . . [Williams's ellipsis]—And being friends is telling each other the truth. . . . [Williams's ellipsis](*There is a pause.*) You told *me!* I told *you!*" The monosyllables of the last two sentences are cutting, like a shamefaced child finding an excuse for hurtful behavior to a parent.

Thematically, the play contrasts Big Daddy's and Brick's insistence on telling the truth with the deception practiced by the doctor, the preacher, Gooper and Mae, and even Maggie. The imagery of game playing enhances both the atmosphere of deception and the theme that time cannot be outraced. In the earlier short story "Three Players of a Summer Game," the game is croquet, which Williams uses in the story both for a boyhood event in the life of the narrator and as an image when he reconstructs the story as an adult, putting together incidents from the past, just as the croquet "paraphernalia" are gathered and packed into a box, "which they just exactly fit and fill." [13] In a larger sense all the characters are players in a deadly serious game, as Williams suggests when he says the focus of the drama is not on the predicament of Brick but, instead, on the group as it faces a crisis.

Sound effects in the play remind us of games: one hears the sounds of croquet being played on the lawn below the windows at the rear. The click of the ball against the mallet may be related to the click Brick hears in his head as a signal of peace and to the click of the phone when he hung up on Skipper. Games and sports recur as images in the play—football, track, childhood games. Maggie's voice, says Williams at the beginning of act 1, "sometimes . . . drops low as a boy's and you have a sudden image of her

CAT ON A HOT TIN ROOF

playing boys' games as a child." The track and hurdles, on which Brick has been injured, Big Daddy sees in act 2 as a sexual game: "I thought maybe you were chasin' poon-tang on that track an' tripped over something in the heat of the chase." Brick replies, "Those high hurdles have gotten too high for me, now."

But time is the real winner in any contest. When he is alone with Big Daddy later in act 2 Brick acknowledges that "time just outran me, Big Daddy—got there first." He says, "Maggie declares that Skipper and I went into pro-football after we left 'Ole Miss' because we were scared to grow up . . . —Wanted to—keep on tossing—those long, long!— high, high!—passes that—couldn't be intercepted except by time" (Williams's ellipsis). Big Mama concludes the game imagery in the last act, recalling Brick playing "wild games" as a child and then reflecting: "Time goes by so fast. Nothin' can outrun it. Death commences too early—almost before you're half-acquainted with life—you meet with the other. . . ." (Williams's ellipsis).

The published text includes two versions of the third act, the act as originally written for production, followed by a "Note of Explanation," and "Act Three as Played in New York Production." Williams's note reveals that director Elia Kazan, with whom the author had worked three times (*Streetcar, Camino Real,* and this play) "had definite reservations" about the third act. He felt that Big Daddy was too "vivid and important" to disappear after the second act, that

Brick "should undergo some apparent mutation as a result of the virtual vivisection that he undergoes in his interview with his father" in act 2, and that Maggie should be "more clearly sympathetic to an audience."

After agreeing about Maggie, Williams explains: "I didn't want Big Daddy to reappear in act three and I felt that the moral paralysis of Brick was a root thing in his tragedy, . . . because I don't believe that a conversation, however revelatory, ever effects so immediate a change in the heart or even conduct of a person in Brick's state of spiritual disrepair. However, I wanted Kazan to direct the play, and . . . I was fearful that I would lose his interest if I didn't re-examine the script from his point of view." Williams adds, generously, "The reception of the playing-script has more than justified, in my opinion, the adjustments made." Four years later Williams was to remark in an article in *Playbill,* "A director of serious plays must learn to accept the fact that nobody knows a play better than the man who wrote it."[14]

In examining tragic implications of the play, Robert Heilman points out that in the Broadway version, in which Brick seems to be undergoing a conversion, if he also could admit to himself his own guilt for Skipper's death (instead of blaming Maggie), this acknowledgment could make Brick a tragic hero, a "divided man" rather than one lacking "conflicting drives."[15]

CAT ON A HOT TIN ROOF

With the third act revised to suit Kazan, the play opened on 24 March 1955 and ran for 694 performances, garnering a Pulitzer Prize and a New York Drama Critics' Circle Award. The reviews were generally good, except for those by critics such as Eric Bentley, who rarely said anything favorable about Williams or his plays. Brooks Atkinson of the *New York Times* wrote approvingly: "Seldom has there been a play in which the expression of thought and feeling has been so complete.... Although Mr. Williams is writing about hidden motivations and other elusive impulses, he is extraordinarily articulate. Being crystal-clear in his own mind, he speaks directly and vividly to the mind of the theatergoer." [16] On the other hand, Robert Hatch called the play "a charade that spells 'psychoanalysis.' ... Villainy in the theater is a splendid, stimulating force, but this cold second-rateness seems to me the negation of drama. Where is the suspense, if no soul is worth saving? Sex and death and money preoccupy Williams's characters; in the face of death, the sex is regulated to get the money." [17]

Although the play with its "Broadway" third act was both appreciated and successful, it is clear from the 1990 Broadway revival that the original third act is truer to the characters and to the artistic integrity of the play. It was directed by Howard Davies, who also had directed it with a different cast at the Royal National Theatre of Great Britain.

In the revised Broadway version of act 3, as the truth
about Big Daddy's condition is about to be revealed to Big
Mama, there is some foreshadowing of the end as Maggie
tells Brick, "I'm goin' to take every dam' bottle on this
place an' pitch it off th'levee into th' river!" A storm is
invented to echo the storm onstage—the kind of theatrical
effect Kazan favored. At Big Mama's words to Brick that
Big Daddy's "fondest dream come true" would be that
Brick would "give him . . . a grandson as much like his son
as his son is like Big Daddy," Big Daddy appears. He tells
a coarse joke with asides to Brick, who inexplicably has
changed into a cheering section. Esther Jackson, who is
evidently basing her observation on the revised version,
feels that "the gradual change reflected in Brick . . . seems
. . . to represent a resolution which is primarily Christian." [18]

Maggie kneels before Big Daddy and makes a speech
considerably extended from the original: "Announcement
of life beginning! A child is coming, sired by Brick, and out
of Maggie the Cat! I have Brick's child in my body, an'
that's my birthday present to Big Daddy on this birthday!"

Big Daddy leaves "to look over my kingdom before I
give up my kingdom"; Brick defends Maggie to Mae and
Gooper; they exit; Maggie spells out to Brick that "I told a
lie to Big Daddy, but we can make that lie come true"; and
the play ends with the corniest of closing lines, as if written
in Hollywood. Maggie repeats the play's title, "Nothing's
more determined than a cat on a tin roof—is there? Is there,

baby?" Years later Kazan admitted that "Williams . . . knew what he'd written and how he would like it staged. I took liberties with his work to yield to my own taste and my overriding tendencies." [19]

It took thirty-five years to appreciate how much better Williams's original third act served the play in production. The direction by Davies, the ensemble acting of the entire cast, and the setting by William Dudley combined to make the 1990 *Cat* the best major production of a play by Williams up to that time. Several factors were at work. With a long record of experience in directing the classics, experience lacked by Kazan, Davies was able to instruct the actors in preserving the cadence and melody of the poetic lines. He combined sensitivity, respect for the author's intentions, and a sure sense of theater that never departs from or is antithetical to the intrinsic values of the play.

Under Davies's direction the ensemble acting reached heights rarely seen in the American theater, and the entire production set a standard for future productions of Williams's plays. The setting fulfilled Williams's "Notes for the Designer," in which he states that "the room must evoke some ghosts; it is gently and poetically haunted." He calls for "a quality of tender light on weathered wood . . . bringing also to mind the grace and comfort of light, the reassurance it gives, on a late and fair afternoon in summer, the way that no matter what, even dread of death, is gently touched and soothed by it. For the set is the background for a play that deals with human extremities of emotion, and it needs that softness behind it."

Williams directs that "the set should be far less realistic than I have . . . implied. . . . I think the walls below the ceiling should dissolve mysteriously into air; the set should be roofed by the sky; stars and moon suggested by traces of milky pallor, as if they were observed through a telescope lens out of focus." Set designer Dudley followed these instructions almost to the letter (as the original Broadway production did not), adding only weeping willows from the top of the proscenium to the top of the set, where the ceiling "dissolve(s) mysteriously." The moon was a full moon, and the lighting by Mark Henderson contributed to the overall effect sought by Williams of a "fair summer sky that fades into dusk and night."

In the 1958 film version of the play Elizabeth Taylor fails to find the music in Maggie's lines, among her other limitations in interpreting this complex role. She was beautiful and desirable as Maggie, but the vulnerability was missing, and there was never a doubt that she would succeed, against any odds. As Brick, Paul Newman combines sensitivity with manliness and athleticism. The film was directed by Richard Brooks, who also co-authored the screenplay. Williams complained that Brooks "at the end . . . cheats on the material, sweetens it up and makes it all hunky-dory." [20]

CAT ON A HOT TIN ROOF

The epigraph is from Dylan Thomas and the closing lines of the introduction are from Emily Dickinson. The Thomas lines are his plea to his dying father not to "go gentle" but to "rage against the dying of the light!" In his introductory essay, "Person—to—Person," Williams quotes Dickinson's poem "I died for beauty" to illustrate that "the discretion of social conversation, even among friends, is exceeded only by the discretion of 'the deep six,' that grave wherein nothing is mentioned at all." He says he does not wish "to talk to people only about the surface aspects of their lives. . . . I still find it somehow easier to 'level with' crowds of strangers in the hushed twilight of orchestra and balcony sections of theaters than with individuals across a table from me. . . . I want to go on talking to you as freely and intimately about what we live and die for as if I knew you better than anyone else whom you know."

Arthur Miller comments on the universality of *Cat on a Hot Tin Roof:* "In an atmosphere . . . of poetic conflict, in a world that is eternal and not merely this world—it provided more evidence that Williams's preoccupation extends beyond the surface realities of the relationships, and beyond the psychiatric connotations of homosexuality and impotence. In every conceivable fashion there was established a goal beyond sheer behavior. We were made to see, I believe, an ulterior pantheon of forces and a play of symbols as well as of characters."[21]

Notes

1. Elia Kazan, *A Life* (New York: Alfred A. Knopf, 1988), 329.

2. *Tennessee Williams: Collected Stories* (New York: New Directions, 1985), 306.

3. Tennessee Williams, "Critic Says 'Evasion,' Writer Says 'Mystery,'" *Where I Live: Selected Essays,* ed. Christine R. Day and Bob Woods (New York: New Directions, 1978), 72–73.

4. Esther Merle Jackson, *The Broken World of Tennessee Williams* (Madison: University of Wisconsin Press, 1965), 63.

5. Arthur Ganz, "A Desperate Morality," in *Tennessee Williams: Modern Critical Views,* ed. Harold Bloom (New York: Chelsea House, 1987), 105.

6. Signi L. Falk, *Tennessee Williams* (New York: Twayne Publishers, 1961), 198.

7. Taped for a broadcast on radio station WBAI-FM New York, by Alice and John Griffin, 29 March 1955.

8. Arthur Waters, "Tennessee Williams Ten Years Later," *Theatre Arts* (July 1955): 73.

9. Johan Huizinga, *Homo Ludens: A Study of the Play-Element in Culture* (London: Routledge and Kegan Paul, 1949), 132.

10. Arthur Miller, "The Shadows of the Gods," *The Theatre Essays of Arthur Miller,* ed. Robert A. Martin (New York: Viking Press, 1978), 190.

11. Tennessee Williams, *Memoirs* (Garden City, N.Y.: Doubleday, 1975), 168.

12. E. Martin Browne, "Editorial Note," *Cat on a Hot Tin Roof* (London: Penguin Books, 1957), 15.

13. Williams, *Collected Stories,* 304.

14. Williams, "Author and Director: A Delicate Situation," in Day and Woods, *Where I Live,* 97.

15. Robert B. Heilman, *The Iceman, the Arsonist, and the Troubled Agent: Tragedy and Melodrama on the Modern Stage* (Seattle: University of Washington Press, 1973), 57–58, 125.

16. Brooks Atkinson, "Cat on a Hot Tin Roof," *New York Times,* 3 April 1955, 2:1

17. Robert Hatch, *Nation* 180, 9 April 1955, 314–15.

18. Jackson, *Broken World,* 58.

19. Kazan, *A Life,* 543.

20. Cecil Brown, "Interview with Tennessee Williams," *Conversations with Tennessee Williams,* ed. Albert J. Devlin (Jackson: University Press of Mississippi, 1986), 275.

21. Miller,"Shadows of the Gods," 190–91.

CHAPTER EIGHT

Orpheus Descending

Orpheus Descending is an intensely human, poetic, and finally tragic picture of the destruction of good by evil. It is Williams's most carefully wrought play. For seventeen years after *Battle of Angels* closed in Boston because of bad reviews, he worked at rewriting it and in 1957 deemed it ready for Broadway. His modern Orpheus is a guitar-playing drifter and the hell he descends into, to defeat death with love, is a mercantile store in a small town, whose prejudice and cruelty destroy him and his beloved. The revised play's title is the same as that of Williams's poem, in which he warns Orpheus:

> And you must learn, even you, what we have
> learned,
> The passion there is for declivity in this world,
> The impulse to fall that follows a rising fountain.[1]

In the myth Orpheus descends into Hades to rescue his beloved Euridice from death's kingdom, where Pluto reigns. The gods grant Orpheus this visit because of the beautiful music he makes with his lyre, music that charms wild beasts. The legend counterpoises transcendence through love with flight from and defeat by death. The theme is a recurrent one in Williams's works. In the play the love of Valentine Xavier and Lady almost triumphs over death, represented by Jabe, proprietor of the underworld, the Torrance Mercantile Store.

After winning back Euridice, only to lose her again as he departs from the underworld, Orpheus meets his death at the hands of maenads, women celebrating a wild bacchic rite. When he rejects them they tear him limb from limb. In the play Jabe and his posse burn Val to death offstage with a blowtorch. In the final scene, as the instrument of death is grabbed from the store and lit, "the men cry out together in hoarse passion crouching toward the fierce blue jet of fire, their faces lit by it like the faces of demons."

As Williams describes his plays as "lyric" and "poetic," one expects symbols. He humorously observes, "Some critics resent my symbols, but let me ask, what would I do without them? Without my symbols I might still be employed by the International Shoe Co. in St. Louis." [2] But his blend of Christian symbols with ones mythic and pagan evoked criticism from those who might have appreciated that the same mixture characterized medieval and Renaissance art, architecture, and literature. Xavier sounds like *savior;* Christ also descended into hell; in *Battle of Angels* Val is killed on Good Friday. Resurrection, one of the themes of the play, is symbolized by the flowery confectionery, which is to open on Easter eve and is Lady's loving recreation of her father's wine garden. Fruitfulness and hope are represented by Lady's conception and by the barren fig tree that finally bears. The Eden-like gold tree with scarlet fruit is a reminder of the Fall of Man. The title of the first version of the play, *Battle of Angels,* refers to the battle in heaven between good and evil angels, resulting in the fall of Lucifer, who becomes the ruler of hell.

Those who hunt after Freudian imagery are never disappointed by Williams: the "phallic guitar is an obvious symbol," [3] one that is "clutched at by sexually undernourished wives of 'small planters,' stroked by the doomed aristocrat seeking death through sex, and threatened by the penis-envying husbands of the community." [4] "Val's guitar," writes Henry Popkin, "has a phallic significance, for the jealous, sexually unsuccessful townsmen approach Val with knives drawn as if to castrate him." [5] The more apparent Freudian images include Williams's omnipresent Moon Lake, here the scene of Romano's wine garden and the artificial trees in the store—the palm on the landing and the gold tree on the curtain of the alcove, itself a symbol.

The many allusions and symbols give added dimension to a plot that builds in dramatic intensity and to characters who are unforgettably vivid. The structure of the action is again that of the visit, as in the myth: Val / Orpheus arrives at the Torrance Mercantile Store / underworld; he finds his love; he hesitates, loses his loved one to death, departs, and is killed.

According to Williams's introductory essay to the play, "The Past, the Present, and the Perhaps," there are "four major protagonists,"—Val, Lady, Vee, and Carol—who continue to ask "unanswered questions that haunt the hearts of people," while the rest of the community accepts "prescribed answers that are not answers at all, but expedient adaptations or surrender to a state of quandary." They accept without question that "people are bought and sold in this world." The mercantile establishment that is the setting for the play metaphorically represents this world as well as the underworld.

Because they question and rebel rather than accept, the four are outsiders, "the fugitive kind," fleeing from the hell created by the townspeople and attempting to outrun the ravages of time. For Williams's heroes and heroines desire, love, conception, liquor, and madness are some of the avenues of escape or transcendence from the imprisonment of life and the inevitability of defeat by time or death.

Lady is another star in Williams's galaxy of women, whose members are so carefully and convincingly drawn that they seem to take on lives of their own, to exist as individuals outside the play. Despite her long and loveless marriage to Jabe, her nervousness and her insomnia, Lady has spirit. Even though she accepts his put-downs and runs upstairs when he knocks on the bedroom floor for her, she channels her energies into the confectionery, patterned after her father's lost wine garden. As a businesswoman, she regards the confectionery as a viable enterprise and can be tough and brusque on this level, although she defers to Jabe. She is a stranger in the midst of the townspeople, a foreigner who was brought from Italy by her father, known in town as "the Wop." His wine garden had prospered during prohibition, but, when he stepped out of line and sold liquor to blacks, the vigilantes of the town, led by Jabe (a fact unknown to Lady), set fire to the vineyards and wine garden. Her father, who died in the fire, had "sold" her to Jabe when Lady was a girl of eighteen, after her lover, society scion David Cutrere, had rejected her.

With great delicacy Williams develops Lady's trans-formation from a suspicious, tough, loveless woman to a loving one, a resurrection of the joyous, singing young girl of the wine garden. From the first time Val threatens to quit, after she rebukes him at a customer's request, to their handshake when he agrees to stay, to Lady's invitation to Val to sleep in the store's dressing alcove instead of a motel, the physical and verbal tension grows between them until the inevitable union at the end of the second act, in the alcove behind the prophetic curtain.

Like Maggie and Amanda, Lady is determined not to be beaten down by life. At the end of the first scene of act 2 she meets David Cutrere for the first time in the years since he "quit" her and tells him: "I—carried your child in my body . . . but I had it cut out. . . . And don't pity me neither. I haven't gone down so terribly far in the world. I got a going concern in this mercantile store, in there's the confectionery."

Her determination "just not to be defeated" by Jabe, the figure of death, culminates in her elation in the final scene when she learns she is pregnant with Val's child: "I've won, I've won, Mr. Death, I'm going to bear!" But her triumph is short-lived, as Jabe, revolver in hand, appears on the landing.

Val's role is the more difficult to interpret onstage, as it is he who combines mythic and realistic qualities; the actor must be entirely convincing on the everyday level yet convey the universal. Val is an artist, a creator of music that affects only those attuned to it—Lady, Carol, and Vee. The mean-spirited world that surrounds him prefers the mechanical jukebox. Like Lady, he is an outsider: she is a foreigner, he a drifter. Both are viewed with apprehension by the townspeople, whose least reaction is to suspect what they cannot understand but who are poised for violence against what they interpret as a threat to their narrow world. Once the Sheriff and his men menace Val after his encounter with Vee in act 3, scene 2, the note of doom is struck, and the tension mounts steadily to the inevitable conclusion.

Val arrives at the Torrance Mercantile Store on his thirtieth birthday; he has hitherto lived a "wild" life selling skins, first those of trapped animals and then his own. Although he seems otherworldly in some respects, he has seen life at its seamiest, as he informs Lady in act 1, scene 2: "Lady, there's just two kinds of people, the ones that are bought and the buyers!" He says he left the bayou where he grew up and at fifteen went to New Orleans, where "I learned that I had something to sell besides snakeskins and other wild things' skins I caught on the bayou. I was corrupted!" But his guitar, his "life's companion," he says, "washes me clean like water when anything unclean has touched me."

Val's dialogue and his songs contribute to his aura of otherworldliness. Just as the music of the legendary Orpheus charmed the beasts and birds, so Val alludes to them often. The most memorable is his poetic description at the end of act 1, of the bird without legs, one of Williams's best lyrical passages, musical and apt. The diction is simple, almost monosyllabic, but the purity of the words, plus the reiteration, rhythm, and assonance, all combine to create poetic music to which the audience responds with the same rapt attention commanded by the Orpheus of legend:

> You know they's a kind of bird that don't have legs so it can't light on nothing but has to stay all its life on its wings in the sky? That's true. I seen one once, it had died and fallen to earth and it was light-blue colored and its body was as tiny as your little finger. . . . they don't have no legs at all and they live their whole lives on the wing, and they sleep on the wind.

Lady recalls the bird in act 2 scene 4, when she is accusing Val of robbing the cash register: "I was touched by your—strangeness, your strange talk.—That thing about birds with no feet so they have to sleep on the wind?—I said to myself, 'This boy is a bird with no feet so he has to sleep on the wind,' and that softened my fool Dago heart and I wanted to help you . . . . Fool, me!" (Williams's ellipsis).

At that point Val is planning to leave, having won at blackjack with money "borrowed" from the cash register, but Lady pleads with him to stay, "I NEED YOU!!! TO LIVE. . . . TO GO ON LIVING!!!" (Williams's ellipsis). He enters the alcove for the first time; she joins him and closes the curtain, which is lit from behind to reveal its "bizarre design, a gold tree with white birds and scarlet fruit."

Throughout the play Val is warned to leave. In act 2, scene 3, he has premonitions himself: "I don't feel safe in this place, but I—want to stay." Dogs are heard offstage, a "wild baying," and Lady comments, "The chain-gang dogs are chasing some runaway convict." Val responds: "*Run boy! Run fast, brother! If they catch you, you never will run again!*" But offstage sounds tell us the fugitive is caught by the dogs and shot by the men. We hear "a single savage note," which Val interprets: "—the dogs've got him. . . . They're tearing him to pieces!" (Williams's ellipsis). Val's death is forecast by the fugitive's, in a parallel to the end of the mythic Orpheus.

Carol also warns Val, when she reappears in act 2, scene 1, after he has started working in the store: "You're in danger, here, Snakeskin. You've taken off the jacket that said: 'I'm wild, I'm alone!' and put on the nice blue uniform of a convict!" After the Sheriff's warning Val knows he must be gone by sunup but delays in the final scene when the nurse declares that Lady is pregnant with his child. Now even Lady urges him to leave, but, just as she is defeated by death in the person of Jabe, so is Val, for it is Jabe's false accusation that leads the posse to destroy this modern-day Orpheus.

Although the directions seem clear enough and the ending is unmistakable when staged, there is some confusion among scholars about how Val meets his offstage end; he is caught—"(Wild cry back of store)" followed by "GOT HIM!" The men grab the blowtorch and rush out. "Somewhere," according to the stage directions, "there is a cry of anguish. . . . The cry is repeated more terribly than before." At least two accounts relate that Val is torn to pieces by the sheriff's dogs.[6] Others believe that Val, in this play, is lynched, according to one, for his sexuality, not his artistry—"Certainly his occasional renditions . . . on the guitar are not adequate motivation for lynching."[7] As the mythic Orpheus is killed by reveling maenads, so Val, it is claimed, is brought to destruction by such maenads as Vee, Carol, and Lady. That trio, or perhaps the townswomen, are seen to be "harpies . . . those malevolent women who pursue him . . . and who destroy him in a Bacchic orgy." [8]

In his introductory essay Williams describes the earlier play, *Battle of Angels,* as "a lyrical play about memories and the loneliness of them." As a writer, the original Val is more closely identified with the artist, the outsider who is suspect, misunderstood by a society that rejects and finally destroys him. The snakeskin jacket, a reminder both of his difference and his "wildness," is also a symbol of his artistic creation, a part of himself which he can slough off and begin anew. At the end of *Orpheus Descending* this jacket is passed on to another, a symbol of resurrection, or new life, just as after his death the head of Orpheus, saved by the muses, continued to sing. In *Battle of Angels* Val tries desperately to leave, as the pregnant Myra (Lady) restrains him. At least one commentator justifies the attempted desertion as the act of an artist who must "remain wild and unrestricted in all sexual relationships." [9] In the final version, although warned to leave, Val refuses to do so when he learns of Lady's pregnancy.

Val's first name, Valentine, suggests Saint Valentine as well as valentines that express love, an opportunity seized by a lady customer who purchases one from Val and then sends it to him. As mentioned, Xavier, his last name, sounds like *savior,* and he has been interpreted as a Christ figure. Although he descends to the underworld and is a figure of love and compassion, he is based only loosely on conventional Christianity. Williams's conception of Val also may have been influenced by "The Man Who Died," D. H. Lawrence's resurrection story, which was roundly condemned as blasphemy when it was published.

Carol and Vee complete the quartet Williams considers his "major protagonists." Unlike Lady and Val, they are not born outsiders. Carol is from a wealthy family in the community, and Vee is the wife of the Sheriff. They could be respected by the town if they conformed to its mores, but they choose to be different. Carol explains herself in a long monologue to Val in act 1, scene 1. She started as a liberal, but, when she joined protests in behalf of "the colored majority in the county" and wore a potato sack to march to the capitol, she was arrested for "lewd vagrancy." Now she spends her time "showing the 'S.O.B.s' how lewd a 'lewd vagrant' can be." She recognizes Val from an earlier encounter in his wilder days and invites him to go "jooking," which she explains as drinking, driving, dancing to juke boxes in bars, and ending with sex. But Val has changed his ways: "I'm thirty years old and I'm done with the crowd you run with and the places you run to."

Cassandra-like, Carol prophesies danger, as does her prototype in *Battle of Angels,* who actually is named Cassandra. Carol's association with the mystic is enhanced by her acquaintance with Uncle Pleasant, a black "conjure man," part Choctaw Indian, who wears talismans and charms. When so bidden by Carol he gives the Choctaw cry, which Williams describes as "a series of barking sounds that rise to a high sustained note of wild intensity." It is this cry in scene 1 which signals the first appearance of Val, as though, Williams tells us, "the cry had brought him."

Onstage alone, at the end, Carol is brought the snakeskin jacket by Uncle Pleasant: "Oh yes, his snakeskin jacket. I'll give you a gold ring for it.—Wild things leave skins behind them, they leave clean skins and teeth and white bones behind them, and these are tokens passed from one to another, so that the fugitive kind can always follow their kind."

Vee Talbott is the opposite of Carol. Vee is the woman who seems to conform. Wife of the Sheriff, she meekly accepts his rebuffs and suffers in silence when she witnesses the violence he instigates. She retreats to her own world, that of her paintings. Her 'visions' set her apart from the rest of the community, as she tells Val in act 2, scene 2: " I was born, I was born with a caul! A sort of thing like a veil, a thin, thin sort of a web was over my eyes. They call that a caul. It's a sign that you're going to have visions, and I did, I had them!" Their duologue is near classical in its stichomythia:

VAL: You lived in Two River County, the wife of the county Sheriff. You saw awful things take place.

VEE: Awful! Things!
VAL: Beatings!
VEE: Yes!
VAL: Lynchings!
VEE: Yes!
VAL: Runaway convicts torn to pieces by hounds!
VEE: (*This is the first time she could express this horror.*) *Chain-gang dogs!* . . . Tear *fugitives!* . . . —to *pieces.*

Vee's second encounter with Val in scene 2 of act 3 seals his fate and forecasts the end. She enters, blinded by a vision of "the blazing eyes of Christ Risen," whose hand, she says, "*touched* me—*here!*" as she seizes Val's hand and places it on her breast. The Sheriff sees the gesture, and he and his men surround Val threateningly, as word goes out that "Sheriff caught him messin' with his wife." From that point on the tension mounts steadily. With the instinctive sense of theater that Williams acknowledged as his "seventh sense," [10] he increases the intensity of the action to build to an inevitable conclusion.

While the men's reaction to Val is physical, the women of the town would destroy Carol and Lady verbally, through gossip. Beulah's monologue in the prologue, Williams notes, "should be treated frankly as exposition, spoken to [the] audience, almost directly. . . . [and] should set the nonrealistic key for the whole production."

Beulah reveals with relish the scandalous goings-on in the wine garden of the Wop, Lady's father, and reports that Jabe and his men burned the wine garden. She and the others consider Carol "degraded" and "corrupt," although Vee points out in the first scene of act 1 that the women's behavior might "set a better example" than giving "drinkin' parties an' get[ting] so drunk they don't know which is their husband and which is somebody else's." Beulah retorts that Vee is a "public kill-joy."

The exchanges between Val and Lady demonstrate Williams's mastery in depicting sexual tension. Realistic and even humorous on the surface, their scenes reveal sexual signals that are subliminal in the characters, though obvious to the audience.

At their first meeting in scene 2 of act 1 Val is showing Lady the autographs on his guitar:

> (*Her voice is also intimate and soft: a spell of softness between them, their bodies almost touching, only divided by the guitar.*)

LADY: You had any sales experience?

VAL: All my life I been selling something to someone.

LADY: So's everybody. You got any character reference on you?

VAL: I have this—letter.

The tension between Lady and Val builds in act 2, which begins with her dismissing (and then rehiring) him because of a valentine-buying customer's complaint:

> LADY: Did you stand in front of her like that? That close? In that, that—*position?*
> VAL: What position?
> LADY: Ev'rything you do is suggestive!
> VAL: Suggestive of what?
> LADY: Of what you said you was through with— somethin'—. . . . My nerves are all shot to pieces. (*Extends hand to him.*) Shake.
> VAL: You mean I ain't fired, so I don't have to quit?

By the end of the act she has invited him to sleep in the store's dressing room alcove; to help her relax he has manipulated her head, neck, and spine—"some tricks I learned from a lady osteopath that took me in, too"—and she has fired him again when she discovers cash missing from the register.

Val has replaced the money, explaining, "I took out less than you owed me."

> LADY: Don't mix up the issue. I see through you, mister!
> VAL: I see through you, Lady.

LADY: What d'you see through me? . . .

VAL: —A not so young and not so satisfied woman, that hired a man off the highway to do double duty without paying overtime for it. . . . [Williams's ellipsis] I mean a store clerk days and a stud nights, and—

Lady tries to strike him, they struggle, he "seizes her wrists" then "lets go of her gently," as she sobs. He starts to leave, she pleads with him to stay, he enters the alcove and takes up his guitar. As the act ends, she pauses before it, "frozen with uncertainty, a conflict of feelings, but then he begins to whisper the words of a song so tenderly that she is able to draw the curtain open and enter the alcove."

Val's speech demonstrates Williams's technique of making poetic dialogue sound realistic. Val's lines, even when he is not singing to his guitar, are the most lyric and musical in the play, as is fitting for a modern Orpheus, albeit an uneducated child of nature. There is balance ("not so . . . not so"; "store clerk days . . . stud nights") and alliteration ("hired . . . highway"; "do double duty"; "store . . . stud") to give a musical and rhythmic effect to what seems to be an ordinary sentence.

He will use repetition: "I lived in corruption but I'm not corrupt"; and metaphors that are apt and imaginative, as in act 2, scene 1: "Nobody ever gets to know *no body!* We're all of us sentenced to solitary confinement inside our own skins, for life!" (He had served time in jail.) Then he describes his life as a child on the bayou, "after my folks all scattered away like loose chicken's feathers blown around by the wind." His reference from a former employer, read by Lady at their first meeting, says: "[He] is a peculiar talker and that is the reason I got to let him go." The poetic effect of Val's dialogue also prepares us for the lyric, onomatopoeic speech about the bird, conveying the feeling of floating on the wind. The folklike lyrics to "Heavenly Grass," the song Val sings at the end of act 2, are from Williams's poem of the same name:

> My feet took a walk in heavenly grass.
> All day while the sky shone clear as glass.
> . . . .
> Then my feet come down to walk on earth,
> And my mother cried when she give me birth.
> Now my feet walk far and my feet walk fast,
> But they still got an itch for heavenly grass.[11]

Lady's characteristic diction combines clichés from the business and social worlds around her; her speech is mostly monosyllabic. Yet she responds to Val's poetry about the bird: "I don't think nothing living has ever been that free, not even nearly." Her humor is tinged with the cynicism of a survivor as she hires Val at the end of act 1: "—Of course I know you're crazy, but they's lots of crazier people than you are still running loose and some of them in high positions, too. Just remember. No monkey business with me. Now go. Go eat, you're hungry."

Even the townspeople have their own idiom. In the prologue Beulah's reminiscing about the wine garden of Lady's father illustrates Williams's technique of heightening the rhythm, repetition, and even the clichés of natural speech to poetically create a mood and to reveal character: "The Wop had took to bootleggin' like a duck to water! . . . he covered the whole no'th shore of the lake with grapevines and fruit trees, and then he built little arbors, little white wooden arbors . . . to drink in and carry on in. . . . And in the spring . . . young couples would come out there . . . we used to go out there, an' court up a storm."

Carol's and Vee's dialogue emphasizes their difference from the other local citizens. Carol's speeches center on herself—her background, her actions, her recollections of former meetings with Val, her frank invitations to him. Vee's dialogue is the more subtly revealing, both in her somewhat breathless speech (she is described as "heavy") and in her recounting of visions, as well as her paintings, all manifestations of sexual frustration.

Jabe, the figure of Death, says very little and is represented mostly by his knocking on the floor for Lady, the rhythmic thuds a harbinger of doom. At the end of the play, when he appears on the landing, revolver in hand, and "peers, crouching, down into the store's dimness to discover his quarry," it is significant that the two words he utters as he shoots are "Buzzards! Buzzards!" The words are those of a hunter spotting game. They express his attitude toward Lady and Val: to Jabe they have no more value than the birds he shoots. Traditional images of death, buzzards are birds of prey that pounce upon and devour stricken victims. The ugly appearance of buzzards and the cacophonous sound of the very words contrast with the beauty of the wingless blue bird of Val's poetic aria.

Of the two Broadway productions of *Orpheus Descending,* the first in 1957 and Peter Hall's in 1989, the second more fully realized the play's values. As noted earlier, Williams's plays suffered from the realistic style that dominated the commercial theater of the 1950s. Despite an understanding producer, Robert Whitehead, and a reputable director who was also a fine critic, Harold Clurman, the original production missed the mark. For Williams's plays the times were out of joint. Clurman's experience as a director was rooted in the realistic Group Theater of the 1930s. If ever plays demanded acting that was larger than life, it was Williams's, but the actors and directors were not to be found. As Williams frequently explained, "Art is compressed and there has to be exaggeration in art form to catch the outrageousness of reality, because art has less time in which to capture it . . . the truth is more accessible when you ignore realism. . . . Exaggeration gets closer to the essence." [12]

As Williams was rewriting the play from *Battle of Angels,* he had Anna Magnani in mind for Lady and, for

Val, probably Marlon Brando, who had created a galvaniz-
ing Stanley in *Streetcar* just ten years earlier. Both stars had
a "larger-than-life" quality that the play needed. They
would appear in the film version, but neither was working
on the stage any longer. As did most directors, Clurman
drew his cast from the Actors' Studio, the descendent of the
Group Theater, choosing Maureen Stapleton to play Lady.
Cliff Robertson was Val, of whose performance Williams
writes, "This was not it at all." [13]

Boris Aronson's set was too realistic and did not
conform to Williams's stage directions, especially the
confectionery, which he describes as "shadowy and poetic
as some inner dimension of the play." It is obviously a
symbol of Lady's happy past in her father's wine garden,
where she and David made love; yet, just as remembered
events can never return, her re-creation of it is artificial—
an "electric moon" and "cut-out silver-paper stars" in a
"paper vineyard" that is "spectral." It frames Lady as she
dies, pointing to "the ghostly radiance of her make-believe
orchard," and, entering it, she "looks about it as people look
for the last time at a loved place they are deserting."

Williams's frequent use of an area within that of the
main action might have been influenced by the Elizabethan
inner stage. The confectionery, like the street activities
seen through the lighted rear wall in *Streetcar* and the
cubicles in *Night of the Iguana,* which Williams compares
to inner stages, all set off an area to provide an "inner
dimension" to the play. Also suggesting a stage-within-a-

stage are the portieres that are drawn and opened between rooms to frame an interior scene in *The Glass Menagerie,* in which Williams calls them "a second curtain."

The large storefront window in the original production of *Orpheus Descending* was neither prominent enough to reveal the weather and happenings outside nor poetic enough to represent a window on hell, as Williams suggests. For the final scene Williams directs that "the view from the great front window has virtually become the background of the action. . . . A lamp outside the door sometimes catches a figure that moves past with mysterious urgency, calling out softly and raising an arm to beckon, like a shade in the under kingdom."

Orpheus Descending opened on 21 March 1957 and lasted only sixty-eight performances. In the *New York Times* the next morning Brooks Atkinson judged it, surprisingly, "one of Mr. Williams's pleasantest plays, with characters determined to free themselves from corruption." But the majority of critics were unkind; Williams describes the "failure" of the play as "a truly shattering setback. . . . The reviewers could have seen its passages of lyric eloquence and permitted themselves to give the play a break. This they chose not to do." [14]

The film went into production two years later in the summer of 1959, with the leading actors Williams originally wanted, Anna Magnani and Marlon Brando. Joanne Woodward was Carol and Vincent Jory, Jabe. Williams himself (with Meade Roberts) wrote the screenplay, and Sidney Lumet directed. In l961, in an article in *Life* magazine, Williams would reveal why, at the time of filming,[15] he had been so reticent about Brando's performance:

> Anna and I had both cherished the dream that her appearance in the part I created for her . . . would be her greatest triumph to date. . . . But Mr. Brando comes at a higher price in more ways than one, especially for a foreign co-player, still unsure of the language. Brando's offbeat timing and his slurred pronunciation were right for the part but they were torture for Anna who had to wait and wait for her cue, and when she received it, it would sometimes not be the one in the script. *The Fugitive Kind* is a true and beautiful film, in my opinion, but mutilated by that uncontrollable demon of competitiveness in an actor too great, if he knew it, to resort to such self-protective devices.[16]

As Williams complains, Brando actually changed the dialogue, which is especially unforgivable in the "bird" speech. Williams observes in *Memoirs* that Clurman "underdirected" the play, but in the film Lumet overdirected Lady and Val, who move so slowly and deliberately that all tension is lost. The end of the film loses not only the impact of the play but, more important, its mythic overtones. Here, repeating the destruction of the original wine garden, Jabe sets fire to the confectionery. He then shoots Lady, not in the store, as she attempts to protect Val, but on the stairs, and accuses Val of the shooting. The Sheriff and his men use fire hoses to force Val into the conflagration, destroying him by fire and water.

A production truer to the script, and one Williams would surely have enjoyed had he been alive, was the 1989 revival on Broadway with Vanessa Redgrave as Lady and Kevin Anderson as Val. Peter Hall, of England's Royal National Theatre, had directed the play in London and then brought the production to Broadway. In 1990 the production was filmed and shown on the Turner television network (TNT).

Williams says in his introductory essay that "it is a very old play that *Orpheus Descending* has come out of, but a play is never an old one until you quit working on it and I have never quit working on this one, not even now": "It always stayed on the work bench. . . . I am offering it this season because I honestly believe that it is finally finished. . . . I believe that I have now finally managed to say in it what I wanted to say."

Although Val and Lady go down to defeat, there is empathy for their spirit and their loss. Theirs is the wild spirit Carol mourns for: "This country used to be wild, the men and women were wild and there was a wild sort of sweetness in their hearts, for each other, but now it's sick with neon." Like Orpheus and Euridice, through the power of love, they almost defeat the dark forces of the under-kingdom before they themselves are defeated. Williams, notes Ingrid Rogers, "seeks to establish a lasting tie between different individual worlds and to let the knowledge of this bond, created in the spectator while he watches the play, be carried into the world." [17]

Notes

1. Tennessee Williams, "Orpheus Descending," *In the Winter of Cities* (Norfolk, Conn.: New Directions, 1956), 28.

2. Tennessee Williams, "A Summer of Discovery," *Where I Live: Selected Essays,* ed. Christine R. Day and Bob Woods (New York: New Directions, 1978), l42.

3. Arthur Ganz, "A Desperate Morality," in *Tennessee Williams: Modern Critical Views,* ed. Harold Bloom (New York: Chelsea House, 1987), l09.

4. Nancy M. Tischler, "The Distorted Mirror: Tennessee Williams's Self-Portraits," *Mississippi Quarterly* 25 (Fall 1972): 392.

5. Henry Popkin, "The Plays of Tennessee Williams," *Tulane Drama Review* 4 (Spring 1960): 6l.

6. Benjamin Nelson, *Tennessee Williams: The Man and His Work* (New York: Ivan Obolensky, 1961), 228; and Beate Hein Bennett, "Williams and European Drama: Infernalists and Forgers of Modern Myths," in *Tennessee Williams: A Tribute,* ed. Jac Tharpe (Jackson: University Press of Mississippi, 1977), 446.

7. Tischler, "Distorted Mirror," 392.

8. Ibid.

9. Norman J. Fedder, *The Influence of D. H. Lawrence on Tennessee Williams* (The Hague: Mouton, 1966), 69.

10. Cecil Brown, "Interview with Tennessee Williams," in *Conversations with Tennessee Williams,* ed. Albert J. Devlin (Jackson: University Press of Mississippi, 1986), 276.

11. Williams, "Heavenly Grass," *In the Winter of Cities,* 101.

12. Brown, "Interview," 264.

13. Tennessee Williams, *Memoirs* (Garden City, N.Y.: Doubleday, 1975), 173.

14. Ibid., 172–73.

15. Interview with author, Milton, N.Y., film location, 26 July 1959.

16. Williams, "Five Fiery Ladies," *Where I Live,* 129–30.

17. Ingrid Rogers, *Tennessee Williams: A Moralist's Answer to the Perils of Life* (Frankfurt: Peter Lang, 1976), 240.

CHAPTER NINE

Sweet Bird of Youth

Sweet Bird of Youth is Williams's most eloquent expression of his recurrent theme that time is "the enemy." In the face of time's relentless advance, transient youth takes flight, deserting those who trusted it. In one of the finest examples of Williams's plastic theater the theme pervades not only the characterization but also the words and action, as well as the setting and sound. It is a forceful and compassionate drama of one decisive day in the lives of a man and a woman played out against a background of sleazy politics and impending violence in a small Southern town.

The female lead is a Hollywood star who reluctantly retired when her youth and beauty faded. While traveling incognito, she changes her name from Alexandra Del Lago to Princess Kosmonopolis, from Williams's recurring symbolic rural lake to the city and Cinderella's ultimate title. Her twenty-nine-year-old male escort is to suffer shock after shock as he comes to realize that appearance and youth, on which he has staked his life so far, must inevitably go down to defeat by "the enemy, time." Gambling on his good looks, he expected to achieve fame and fortune in the movies and so far has gone from bit parts to beach boy, encouraged by what Williams sees as "the Cinderella story

. . . our favorite national myth, the cornerstone of the film industry, if not of the Democracy itself." [1] Appropriately, his name is Chance.

The play, like others by Williams, takes the form of a visit. The action begins with the couple's arrival on Easter Day, implying hope. But by the end only despair is left for Chance. As the play opens, they have checked in at "a fashionable hotel somewhere along the Gulf Coast, in a town called in St. Cloud," Chance's hometown, where in high school he was a "star."

Act 1 takes place in their hotel suite, where literally and figuratively circling each other, Chance and the Princess reveal the immediate and distant past, which brought them to the present instant. She is traveling in style, fleeing from failure. So shocked was she at her appearance in close-up at her comeback film's premiere that she ran up the aisle and out of the theater, in "interminable retreat from the city of flames." She seeks refuge in drink, drugs, and sex. Chance has made this detour on his trip with the Princess to show off in his hometown the expensive clothes, the Cadillac, and the acting contract the Princess has signed with him during their journey, "notarized and witnessed by three strangers found in a bar." Besides Hollywood stardom Chance has another impossible dream, to marry his hometown sweetheart, Heavenly, his "one true love," whose father has other ideas for her future.

In some ways the Princess represents Chance's dream of fame, although even he can see that she is far from happy, but she has one thing Chance lacks—talent. Chance brags that he had won an acting contest; the truth is that he received only honorable mention. Yet his illusions of stardom may be realized by means of the contract, which he will attempt to enforce by blackmailing the Princess after he has secretly tape-recorded her using drugs. But age and experience will be on her side. She is a survivor. Chance, who has only his youth and good looks, is destined to be a victim of time.

As the Princess lies asleep, a mask over her eyes blotting out the reality she cannot face, the first caller at their suite is young Doctor Scudder. He warns Chance to leave town; as a "criminal degenerate," he is threatened with castration for infecting "a certain girl," who is now engaged to the doctor. Although Chance and Heavenly have been lovers since high school, her father will allow her to marry only if the man is wealthy. This has led to Chance's pursuit of easy money as a gigolo to rich women, but he has gained nothing but a venereal disease. Unknowingly, he has transmitted it to Heavenly. The events of the day and the relationship with the Princess destroy Chance's dreams and teach him the bitter lesson that his youth will desert him as he reaches the noon of his life.

The Princess and Chance are among Williams's best character creations. She recognizes that she is a "monster," but she has confidence in her talent. She also is realistic about the ravages of time, recognizing the transience of her comeback (which she is to learn later has been successful).

She is imperious, tough, self-indulgent, vulnerable, and alone. She tries to reach out when she feels some stirring in her heart for Chance, and there is the hope of caring companionship, if not love, between them. But when he rejects her she realizes that she is, and always will be, a loner. She knows she has to make it alone; she is not dependent on "the kindness of strangers." (Although one commentator classifies her with "women who have known happiness but who have lost their mates and who try to overcome the loss," [2] there seems to be little justification for this in the text.)

The Princess is aware, as Williams points out in his stage directions, that "the clock is equally relentless to them both." Her long aria in act 1 explains that she retired from films because her looks were fading and her youth was gone, but she was still "unsatisfied and raging":

> PRINCESS: . . . If I had just been old but you see, I wasn't old. . . .
> I just wasn't young, not young, young.
> I just wasn't young anymore. . . .
> CHANCE: Nobody's young anymore. . . .
>   (all Williams's ellipses)

The play's change of setting and shift of emphasis between acts 1 and 2 had its critics and its defenders. As Walter Kerr wryly observes, "*Sweet Bird of Youth* was . . . quickly popular, and quickly attacked. Many things were

said: that the political second act was the *real* play and
should have been developed, that the personal story of the
first and third acts constituted the *real* play and that the
second should have been omitted." [3] While Benjamin Nelson
criticizes the play's "blatant lack of unity" and claims that
"act one has almost nothing to do with act two," [4] careful
observation indicates that act 2 dramatizes conflicts established in act 1, namely between Chance and Boss Finley,
Chance and the peers he left behind, and Chance and the
Princess.

The act is a merciless mirror of small-town prejudice
and its antagonism, rooted in envy, toward Chance. Scene
1 takes place on Boss Finley's plantation, always inaccessible to Chance because he was born on the wrong side of
the tracks, and scene 2 is set in the hotel cocktail lounge
where Chance's former pals, now his enemies, congregate.
Not that Chance's condescending attitude endears him to
these men. A reminder of his high school dreams of
Hollywood stardom is his confiding to the bartender,
whose job Chance formerly held, that he designed the
uniform, based on a costume Victor Mature wore in a
foreign legion film, and, he says, "I looked better in it than
he did."

In scene 2 Williams creates in the cocktail lounge,
almost entirely through offstage effects, all the hoopla and
hype of a political rally. Car sirens, band music, headlights,
and flashbulbs herald Boss Finley's arrival with Tom
Junior and Heavenly, as they march through on their way

to the platform in the ballroom, where Boss will deliver on "all-South-wide TV" his "Voice of God" speech. (A Cinderella figure himself, Boss rose from obscurity to prominence when, he claims, God spoke to him.) He says God told him to take violent action against "all of them that want to adulterate the pure white blood of the South." At the bar Miss Lucy, Boss's mistress, whom he has treated cruelly, protects the Heckler from discovery. When she comments that Boss "honestly believes" God has spoken to him, the Heckler counters: "I believe that the silence of God, the absolute speechlessness of Him is a long, long and awful thing that the whole world is lost because of. I think it's yet to be broken to any man, living or any yet lived on earth,—no exceptions, and least of all Boss Finley."

Then the back wall of the set becomes a huge television screen, with Boss's head filling the screen as he warns of the threat of "blood pollution" from the black race. In counterpoint to the speech Miss Lucy is warning Chance to leave: as punishment for infecting Heavenly, he has been threatened with the same fate as that suffered by a black man apprehended at random—castration.

On the TV screen the camera swings to the Heckler interrupting Boss Finley with a question about Heavenly's operation, then we see Boss trying to quell the outbreak of disturbance, and then, offscreen, the Heckler comes tumbling down the lounge stairs, beaten by Finley's henchmen. In eight minutes of sheer theatricality Williams has left no doubt of the threat to the state and the threat to Chance by the sanctimonious preacher of hate. Although Williams states "social consciousness . . . has marked most of my writing,"[5] and the truth of his remark can be seen in the wider implications of his works, this is the only specific intrusion of politics in the major plays. It dramatizes the dangers inherent in the Boss Finleys who claim God has spoken to them and directs their actions. This climactic scene closes act 2 with political conflict, while act 3 brings to a head the personal conflict between Chance and the Princess.

Williams's seventh sense of theatrical instinct is nowhere so evident as in his reaching a note of high drama as the end approaches. He creates a magic that is so memorable it is forever associated with this play. Chance phones an influential gossip columnist to have the Princess announce him as a "discovery" to star with Heavenly in a new film called *Youth*. Instead, the Princess learns that her movie is not a flop but a hit, "the greatest comeback in the history of the industry." Her transformation from fugitive back into movie queen, in the course of a brief telephone conversation, is pure theater and pure Williams—humorous, lyric, compassionate, and true. It concludes:

CHANCE: Here, get her back on this phone. . . . Talk about me and talk about Heavenly to her.
PRINCESS: Talk about a beach-boy I picked up for

pleasure, distraction from panic? Now? When the
nightmare is over? . . . You've just been using me. . . .
When I needed you downstairs you shouted, 'Get her
a wheel chair!' Well, I didn't need a wheel chair, I
came up alone, as always. . . . Chance, you've gone
past something you couldn't afford to go past; your
time, your youth, you've passed it. It's all you had,
and you've had it.

Chance reacts furiously, forcing her to look at herself
in the mirror, to see that her youth and beauty have gone.
Instead, she says she sees "Alexandra Del Lago, artist and
star!" The difference between her and Chance, she tells
him, is that "out of the passion and torment of my existence
I have created a thing that I can unveil, a sculpture, almost
heroic, that I can unveil, which is true."

But Chance can only wonder why he never got the
chance to make it: "Something's got to mean something,
don't it, Princess? I mean like your life means nothing,
except that you never could make it, always almost, never
quite?"

Chance in some ways resembles Val in *Orpheus Descending.* Both are young men who have chosen the easy
path of "corruption" in life but who, at the ages of twenty-
nine and thirty, feel the pressure of time. Both have a true
love for a woman but are defeated by outside forces—the
small town and its denizens who gang up on Val for a
mistaken breach of conduct and, in *Sweet Bird,* the political

force of Boss Finley, which punishes Chance for a personal reason, being a "criminal degenerate" whose venereal disease, transmitted to Heavenly, has resulted in her hysterectomy. The Heckler, of course, believes the operation to have been an abortion, illegal at that time. Chance is the more complex and human of the two, for, while both young men have fallen prey to corruption, Chance's own misguided ideals bring about his downfall. Unlike a true tragic hero, he never attains a significant recognition—that the fame and fortune he seeks are not inevitably the reward of good looks (especially as Hollywood demonstrates otherwise). The personal truth he does realize at the end, that his youth and attractiveness are fleeting, makes him a pathetic rather than a tragic figure.

Finley's forces are even more deadly than the townspeople in *Orpheus Descending,* for Finley stirs up statewide racial hatred. Because of his political prominence and ambitions, Boss, who never could accept Chance as a son-in-law, is as ruthless in his family relations as in his political aims. Chance's former schoolmates, whose clothes and jobs he derides, form a chorus of men who join forces against him with the sinister Youth for Finley, a kind of junior Ku Klux Klan. They also demonstrate another facet of youth, its group violence. Their brutality is first seen against the Heckler, who is "systematically beaten." Even though the final moments are quiet, their menacing members surround Chance at the end, and we assume he will be castrated, the fate with which he has been threatened.

Williams in his Sunday *New York Times* article of 8 March 1959 (often used as the play's "Foreword"), prior to the opening of *Sweet Bird of Youth*, answers the charge that his plays are violent: "I write about violence in American life only because I am not so well acquainted with the society of other countries. . . . If there is any truth in the Aristotelian idea that violence is purged by its poetic representation on a stage, then it may be that my cycle of violent plays have had a moral justification after all."

In *Sweet Bird of Youth* Williams perfectly achieves his ideal of plastic theater, in which characterization, action, language, setting, and sound create an artistic unity expressing the theme. As always, the dialogue characterizes the speakers. In Williams's large cast of memorable women the Princess has her unique idiom—tough, resilient, decisive, knowing. In act 1, scene 1, she sizes up Chance after he tries to blackmail her: "I hate to think of what kind of desperation has made you try to intimidate me, ME? . . . . You were well born, weren't you? . . . with just one disadvantage, a laurel wreath on your forehead, given too early, without enough effort to earn it." Then she sets forth her terms of employment for Chance in a passage that reminds us that time is even more of an enemy to her, being older than Chance:

Forget the legend that I was and the ruin of that legend. . . . No mention of death, never, never a word on that odious subject. I've been accused of having a death wish but I think it's life that I wish for, terribly, shamelessly, on any terms whatsoever. When I say now, the answer must not be later. I have only one way to forget these things I don't want to remember and that's through the act of love-making.

She can be lyric as well. In act 2, scene 2, after Tom Junior has threatened Chance, she hears a strain of thematic music, which Williams calls "The Lament." She describes time's loss in a passage that creates its own music through assonance, alliteration, onomatopoeia, repetition, and rhythm:

All day I've kept hearing a sort of lament that drifts through the air of this place. It says, 'Lost, lost, never to be found again.' Palm gardens by the sea and olive groves on Mediterranean islands all have that lament drifting through them. 'Lost, lost.'. . . [Williams's ellipsis] The isle of Cyprus, Monte Carlo, San Remo, Torremolenas, Tangiers. They're all places of exile from whatever we loved. . . . Chance, believe me, after failure comes flight. . . . Face it. Call the car.

Unlike Chance, however, she at least has the assurance of her talent as she faces her faded looks in the mirror. Although she is clear-eyed about time, the defeater, she will still go on; as she says monosyllabically to Chance at the end, "Chance, we've got to go on." This motif of going on despite obstacles will be repeated by Hannah, almost verbatim, in *The Night of the Iguana.*

Chance's idiom is less distinctive, but Williams's artistry heightens what could be the banalities of the less educated. Almost entirely monosyllabic, his speeches are nevertheless sharp, so that the give-and-take with the Princess, which occupies the entire first act, reveals the characters of both. When in scene 1 the Princess asks if he has any acting talent, Chance replies: "I'm not as positive of it as I once was. I've had more chances than I could count on my fingers, and made the grade almost, but not quite, every time. Something always blocks me."

Because Chance and the Princess are on the stage so much of the time, and the portraits of them are so detailed, the other characters are less well developed. Heavenly has very little to say; she is acted upon instead of active, a direct contrast to the Princess. Nonnie, Heavenly's ineffectual but kindly maiden aunt, who is sympathetic to Chance, resembles her counterpart in Williams's film *Baby Doll* and his one-act play *The Unsatisfactory Supper.*

Like Jabe in *Orpheus Descending,* Boss Finley is one of Williams's few characters without redeeming qualities, unless it be his (misguided) love for his daughter. In his one encounter alone with Heavenly, in scene 1 of act 2, there is, "in her father," Williams points out, "a sudden dignity": "It's important not to think of his attitude toward her in the terms of crudely conscious incestuous feeling, but just in the natural terms of almost any aging father's feeling for a

SWEET BIRD OF YOUTH

beautiful young daughter who reminds him of a dead wife that he desired intensely when she was the age of his daughter." Boss's idiom resembles Big Daddy's, in that it is gruff, colorful, and proudly uneducated. In addition, because Boss is not sympathetic, his speeches reflect his sense of power; he is used to giving orders and seeing them obeyed.

When Heavenly suggests that he has "an illusion of power," he replies, "I have power, which is not an illusion." She informs him that, if she is accepted, she is "going into a convent." Boss shouts: "You ain't going into no convent. This state is a Protestant region and a daughter in a convent would politically ruin me."

With great economy but deadly aim and sure theatricalism Williams portrays in Boss Finley the danger of a corrupt, power-hungry politician who will destroy anything that stands in his way and anyone who threatens his public image. The symbol of this image and the danger it implies is the stunning stage effect in scene 2 of act 2, in which the entire back wall of the stage becomes an enormous TV screen, on which appears "the image of Boss Finley."

George Brandt believes Williams's cinematic style is illustrated by this scene, which is an attempt "to turn the playhouse into a picture theater." [6] But it should be remembered that Williams had studied theater at the New School with Erwin Piscator, a proponent of the use of back-projected film to achieve stage effects. Piscator's wife,

Maria Ley-Piscator, presents a strong argument for Williams's use of the latter technique.[7]

The epigraph for the play is by Hart Crane, whose work Williams greatly admired: "Relentless caper for all those who step / The legend of their youth into the noon."

It is a warning to "all those" whose hopes depend on the legend of their youth that it will not survive the bright light of the sun when they reach the noon of life. Entitled "Legend," Crane's poem begins: "As silent as a mirror is believed / Realities plunge in silence by."

Constant reminders of the passing of time and of youth are Williams's symbols of the clock and the mirror. At the climax of the play, in act 3, Chance forces the Princess to confront in the mirror the reality of her aging face, a sight she confesses was so terrifying to her when it filled the screen at the preview of her comeback film that she fled: "The screen's a very clear mirror. There's a thing called a close-up. . . . Your head, your face, is caught in the frame of the picture with a light blazing on it and all your terrible history screams while you smile" (act 1, sc. 1). But she is not defeated, for she tells Chance that in the mirror she sees herself as "artist and star," while his mirror image discloses "a face that tomorrow's sun will touch without mercy."

In a rhythmic, onomatopoeic elegy Heavenly also laments the loss of her youth. The operation, she says in scene 1 of act 2, "cut the youth out of my body, made me an old childless woman": "Dry, cold, empty, like an old woman. I feel as if I ought to rattle like a dead dried-up vine when the Gulf Wind blows." And Aunt Nonnie, Chance's only confidant in St. Cloud tells him the truth about his return: "What you want to go back to is your clean, unashamed youth. And you can't."

Despite its lyric dialogue, Williams thought of the action of this play as realistic, yet sudddenly, just before the play ends, it shifts gears. The closing moments are nonrealistic and poetic. In the hotel room—and what can be more transient to reflect time passing?—Chance and the Princess sit side by side on the bed, directly facing the audience, "like two passengers on a train sharing a bench." The metaphor is that of a train trip, a journey through life. The Princess points out sights along the way:

> PRINCESS: . . . Look [Williams's ellipsis]. That little donkey's marching around and around to draw water out of a well. . . .—What an old country, timeless—Look—*(The sound of a clock ticking is heard, louder and louder).*
>
> CHANCE: No, listen. I didn't know there was a clock in this room.
>
> PRINCESS: I guess there's a clock in every room people live in.

A trooper enters, and Tom Junior is at the door. The Princess pleads, "Come on, Chance, we're going to change

trains at this station. . . . So, come on, we've got to go on .
. . . Chance, please. . . ." (both Williams's ellipses). But
Chance shakes his head, and she departs, as he at last
realizes that life is a journey in time and that he is approaching the end of the line.

Yet at the end, with everything gone and violence
imminent, defeated Chance retains his dignity, as he asks:
"Time—who could beat it, who could defeat it ever ?
Maybe some saints and heroes, but not Chance Wayne."
Williams points out in his stage direction that "Chance's
attitude should be self-recognition but not self-pity—a sort
of deathbed dignity and honesty apparent in it." As Tom
Junior and three other men hover in the doorway, ready to
strike, Chance advances to the front of the stage and
addresses the closing lines directly to the audience: "I don't
ask for your pity, but just for your understanding—not even
that—no. Just for your recognition of me in you, and the
enemy, time, in us all."

In the 1959 Broadway premiere Geraldine Page as the
Princess and Paul Newman as Chance were outstanding in
evoking the poetry of the play and in preserving the magic
of the final scene. In a 1945 interview Williams had asserted
that "the poetic theater needs . . . more fine, intuitive actors.
. . . We've gotten into the habit, actors in the Broadway
theater, of talking like parrots. And poetry dies through that
form of delivery.[8]

Although director Elia Kazan did well with the realistic scenes, Page's and Newman's own considerable talents were responsible for realizing the poetry and the magic that made the production memorable. Their familiarity with Williams's characters no doubt helped, as they had already achieved outstanding interpretations as Alma in *Summer and Smoke* and as Brick in the movie version of *Cat on a Hot Tin Roof.* In a role allegedly based on actress Tallulah Bankhead, Page brought out every facet of the part, quick-silver in her changes from imperious to pathetic, from brittle and determined to resigned and caring. Newman was equally impressive as Chance, his underlying desperation perceptible beneath the bravado.

Good newspaper reviews the following morning of ll March led to long lines at the box office, with Brooks Atkinson of the *Times* pronouncing the play one of Williams's "finest dramas." "Williams Drama Attracts Throngs" was the *Times* headline. Magazine reviewers were somewhat more critical. Harold Clurman, commenting on the curtain speech, asked: "What is it we were asked to recognize in ourselves? That we are corrupted by our appetite for the flesh and clamor of success? That we are driven to live debased existences by the constrictions and brutality which surround us? That the sound instincts of our youth are thus frustrated and turned to gall? And that we have an inordinate fear of age, for the passing of time makes us old before we mature?"[9] Marya Mannes deplored the "violence of corruption and decay . . . in which a poet's imagination must feed on carrion."[10] In a more reasoned consideration of the play Robert Heilman feels there is insufficient sympathetic development of the character of Chance, which resembles that of Brick, in that both men experience a "premature glory," which then fades. Interpreting Chance's actions as "so shallow and preposterous that the self-recognition is hardly plausible in terms of character," Heilman wonders how the ending can work, when Chance addresses the audience "like the Doctor in the morality play."[11] But for the audience in the theater the ending *does* work.

The 1962 film, written and directed by Richard Brooks, at least preserves the performances of Geraldine Page and Paul Newman as well as some of Williams's dialogue in their scenes together. Yet the banal new dialogue and the flashback scenes detailing the love affair between Chance and Heavenly (Shirley Knight) reduce the work to an average movie, with an ending that negates the premise. Williams complained that the happy ending was "a total contradiction to the meaning of the play."[12]

Sweet Bird of Youth represents Williams at his best in combining realism, lyricism, and theatricalism. The characters are so realistically drawn, down to the last detail, that their names have become tags for real-life types—a Southern politician who wins votes by appealing to fears of racial discord is a "Boss Finley," a good-looking young man who expects to succeed without talent, a "Chance Wayne." At the same time, Williams's universal theme, expressed in symbolism, stage effects, and heightened speech, unites with his sure sense of theatricality to produce a work that enriched both his reputation and that of the American theater.

Notes

1. Tennessee Williams, "On a Streetcar Named Success," *Where I Live: Selected Essays,* ed. Christine R. Day and Bob Woods (New York: New Directions, 1978), 15.

2. Louise Blackwell, "Tennessee Williams and the Predicament of Women," *South Atlantic Bulletin* 35 (March 1970): 13.

3. Walter Kerr, "Mr. Williams," *The Theatre in Spite of Itself* (New York: Simon and Schuster, 1963), 249.

4. Benjamin Nelson, *Tennessee Williams: The Man and His Work* (New York: Ivan Obolensky, 1961), 266.

5. Williams, "Facts about Me," *Where I Live,* 60.

6. George Brandt, "Cinematic Structure in the Work of Tennessee Williams," *American Theatre* (London: Edward Arnold, 1967), 10:168.

7. Maria Ley-Piscator, *The Piscator Experiment* (New York: James H. Heineman, 1967), 236.

8. George Freedley, "The Role of Poetry in the Modern Theatre" (interview on radio station WNYC, New York, 3

October 1945), in *Conversations with Tennessee Williams,* ed. Albert J. Devlin (Jackson: University Press of Mississippi, 1986), 23.

9. Harold Clurman, "Theater," *Nation* 188, 28 March 1959, 281.

10. Marya Mannes, "Theater," *Reporter* 20, 16 April 1959, 34.

11. Robert B. Heilman, *The Iceman, the Arsonist, and the Troubled Agent: Tragedy and Melodrama on the Modern Stage* (Seattle: University of Washington Press, 1973), 127.

12. Cecil Brown, "Interview with Tennessee Williams," *Conversations with Tennessee Williams,* ed. Albert J. Devlin (Jackson: University Press of Mississippi, 1986), 275.

CHAPTER TEN

The Night of the Iguana

The Night of the Iguana is the last and possibly the best of Williams's major plays, for its celebration of human endurance and dignity, its depiction, according to its author, of the most "complete" and "sympathetic" of his male characters, and its portrayal of the most complex and appealing female in the extensive gallery of Williams's women—Hannah Jelkes. Although its 1961 production barely hinted at the rich and evocative script, it was a hit despite its rocky road to Broadway. In its tryout in Chicago it was judged "a bankrupt play," and the director was not only fired but also ordered to leave the city.[1]

Its haunted thirty-five-year-old hero, Reverend Lawrence T. Shannon, on the verge of nervous collapse, arrives at a quiet Mexican hotel. Here he encounters another visitor, Hannah Jelkes, a spinster of forty who is equally desperate but otherwise almost totally his opposite. During the course of a night in the Eden-like setting of the Costa Verde, high above a still water beach, they will display "the humble nobility of each putting the other's desperation . . . above his concern for his own."[2]

Ten years earlier Shannon's congregation had locked him out of the church because of "fornication and heresy . . . in the same week" (Williams's ellipsis), he confesses to Hannah in act 2. He seduced a young parishioner and in the following Sunday sermon challenged "Western theologies" because they "accuse God of being a cruel, senile delinquent, blaming the world and brutally punishing all he created for his own faults in construction."

After leaving his parish, Shannon conducted prestigious round-the-world tours, but indulgence in sex and drink has brought him to the lowest level of the tour hierarchy: "I lose this job, what's next? There's nothing lower than Blake Tours," he laments on his arrival. Exhausted, haunted by a "spook," he has brought his Mexican tour party of Baptist college women to the Costa Verde Hotel, owned by his old friends, Fred and Maxine. Maxine, who is now running the hotel with the help of two virile young Mexicans, greets Shannon with the news of Fred's death.

Exposition is expertly woven into the action of the opening scene, in which Shannon (who has forcibly stopped the tour bus at the nonscheduled hotel) is pursued and threatened by a fierce member of the tour, Judith Fellowes, made all the more fierce by Shannon's recent seduction of a willing teenager in the group.

As Shannon and Miss Fellowes clash, Hannah Jelkes arrives. Williams's most admirable female character, she is developed from his 1948 short story of the same name as the play. Edith is the central figure in the story, in which Shannon does not appear. The transformation from the weaker, Blanche-like Edith to Hannah is a fascinating view of Williams's artistry at work. Hannah is a woman of courage and compassion, despite the fact that she, like Shannon, is in desperate straits, traveling without funds, at rest only briefly before forcing herself to continue.

Maxine Faulk completes this unusual triangle. Described as "a stout, swarthy woman in her middle forties—affable and rapaciously lusty," she does her best to help Shannon out of his attack—and into her bed. Shannon must parry her advances while playing for the time he needs at the hotel to regain his composure and then to resume his journey. But his seduction of teenaged Charlotte has added urgency to his plight. The conflict with Miss Fellowes escalates as she phones Texas to bring legal charges against Shannon.

All three characters in the triangle—Maxine, Shannon, and Hannah—are fully and deeply explored. Maxine, who welcomes Shannon affably, senses a threat when Hannah arrives and is immediately hostile to her. Despite Hannah's protest that she is "a New England spinster," Maxine warns her at the end of act 2: "You're not for Shannon and Shannon isn't for you. . . . I got the vibrations between you . . . and there sure was a vibration between you and Shannon the moment you got here." The growing affinity between Shannon and Hannah is as unique as it is convincing.

On the periphery of the action is Hannah's grandfather Nonno, once known as a minor poet, now "ninety-seven years *young.*" He has cared for Hannah since she was orphaned as a child, and now she cares for him as they travel the resorts of the world, where he recites his poetry and she sketches indulgent tourists to earn a livelihood. Depending on the kindness of strangers, she passes among the hotel tables at lunch or dinner, smiling, dressed in an artist's smock "picturesquely dabbed with paint," displaying her water colors, and, if asked to sit down, does so, to make a "quick character sketch." They have no fixed address, but, in her long, third-act conversation with Shannon, Hannah defines a home as "a thing that two people have between them in which each can . . . well, nest—rest—live in, emotionally speaking" (Williams's ellipsis).

Even at his advanced age Nonno is still creative, striving to complete a poem in recited snatches, which Hannah records. He is nearly blind as well as deaf and temporarily immobile, confined to a wheelchair but insisting on traveling to the sea at this locale because, as he announces on arriving in act 1: "It's the cradle of life. Life began in the sea." This remark and the old man's references to himself as a child again reinforce the symbolism of the life cycle. Hannah has pushed his wheelchair (which he refers to as "my perambulator") up the hill to the hotel.

Within the space of a day and a night at the Costa Verde Williams develops the outer conflicts of the characters with such theatricality and their inner conflicts with such understanding that at the conclusion we share his concern for their destinies.

THE NIGHT OF THE IGUANA

While Shannon is aware that he flees from despair and his "spook," he can only express but not understand the deep sense of sin and guilt which afflicts him in sexual matters. At the beginning of act 3 Maxine tells him that she knows his "psychological history," for she once overheard her husband and Shannon, who was speaking of his mother's instilling a sense of guilt in him. When she discovered his "little boy's vice" of masturbation she punished him severely, telling him that she had to do so "because it made God mad as much as it did Mama, and she had to punish [him] for it so God wouldn't punish [him] for it harder than she would." As a result, his mature sexual encounters are always followed by guilt and punishment, as he reports in the incident with the young parishioner. And, as Charlotte recalls in act 2: "I remember that after making love to me, you hit me, Larry, you struck me in the face, and you twisted my arm to make me kneel on the floor and pray with you for forgiveness." Shannon responds, "I do that, I do that always when I, when . . ." (Williams's ellipsis).

In act 2, as Hannah sketches him, Shannon reveals more of his past and present. Although the congregation accused him of "heresy" for attacking the concept of God as cruel and punishing, he is not a disbeliever; rather, as Williams explains, he is "torn between belief and disbelief," just as he is "between sexuality and guilt." [3] "I want to go back to the Church and preach the gospel of God as Lightning and Thunder," he tells Hannah. The impending storm with its thunder and lightning demonstrates his conception of God, as does the magnificence of the sunset: "That's him! There he is now! (*He is pointing out at a blaze, a majestic apocalypse of gold light, shafting the sky as the sun drops into the Pacific.*) His oblivious majesty." When the thunder, lightning, and sheets of rain arrive at the end of the act, Williams creates an unforgettable stage picture, as Shannon reaches out to this display: "Shannon ... stretches [his hands] out through the rain's silver sheet as if he were reaching for something outside and beyond himself. Then nothing is visible but these reaching-out hands." It is a daring, Lear-like, poetic and symbolic image, though Shannon feels he is more sinning than sinned against.

Esther Jackson observes, "It is God his protagonist seeks" in this play, but, when she claims that "Williams's God is the stern but forgiving 'Father' of American Protestantism," it must be noted that this interpretation of a stern God is what Shannon has rebelled against and that he has been driven from his church because of this "heresy."[4] Ingrid Rogers is more convincing when she states that Williams's God is a "God of love, not of cruel revenge."[5] But, while waiting for God to come to the rescue, humans may perform "little acts of grace," such as Shannon's freeing the iguana and Hannah's restoring Shannon by leading him beside the still waters.

The sympathy that Hannah and Shannon share is not to be found in self-centered Maxine. When Hannah and

THE NIGHT OF THE IGUANA

Nonno arrive in act 1 Maxine suspects they are penniless; only Shannon's kind intervention prevents her from turning them away. Both Shannon and Hannah are on journeys, traveling the world, visiting hotels; neither has a permanent home. Both are hustlers, constantly improvising, using all their resources just to survive. When Hannah resolves in act 2 to peddle her watercolors to Shannon's ladies, he observes with admiration, "By God, you're a hustler, aren't you, you're a fantastic cool hustler," to which she replies, "Yes, like *you,* Mr. Shannon."

Both Maxine and Hannah try to help Shannon stave off an impending crack-up. Maxine continually offers Shannon a drink, but he realizes that, in the past, alcohol and sex have afforded only temporary escape from the conflicts that are tearing him apart. At the beginning of act 3 the final straw is a double blow: the appearance of rival Jake to take over the tour and the announcement by Miss Fellowes that she has been successful in barring Shannon from future employment. Despairing, "with an animal outcry," as the tour bus departs, Shannon is about to "swim out to China" (his euphemism for suicide), when Hannah, Maxine, and the Mexican boys tie him into the veranda hammock. Maxine warns that he will be confined to a mental institution if he continues his outrageous behavior.

But it is Hannah who calms him, who talks him through his panic, in their long conversation toward the end of act 3. The breadth of her humanity and understanding is all-encompassing. She even convinces him that the ladies' complaints were justified on the disastrous tour: "After all, they did save all year to make this Mexican tour."She reminds him of a need beyond the physical, "the need to believe in something or in someone—almost anyone— almost anything . . . something" (Williams's ellipsis). She has two trump cards to play to insure he survives the night and his attack. One is a confession of her own near break- down and how she overcame her "blue devil": "I showed him that I could endure him and I made him respect my endurance."

The other trump card is her response when he asks, "Have you never had in your life any kind of a lovelife?" She relates the episode with the salesman so delicately that it not only exemplifies her extraordinary compassion, but it may help resolve Shannon's anxiety. In response to his perception of the event as "sad" and "dirty," she regards it as human: "Nothing human disgusts me unless it's unkind, violent." With her unique insight, which finds a positive in every seeming negative, Hannah helps Shannon to see and face truths about himself.

The Costa Verde, to which Shannon retreats when the world is too much for him, is set back in time to 1940, before it was developed, "and the still-water morning beach of Puerto Barrio and the rain forests above it were among the world's wildest and loveliest populated places," recalls Williams, in describing the setting at the beginning of the play. His Sunday article before the play's opening recounts in fuller detail the actual Costa Verde hotel and his month-long experiences there in the 1940s, the time of the play.[6]

Alongside this paradise there is an evil underside of the tropics. Shannon is acutely aware of its heart of darkness, its "horrors" he has forced the tour ladies to see along with the customary sights: "It's always been tropical countries I took ladies through," he reflects during his conversation with Hannah in act 3. "Fast decay is a thing of hot climates, steamy, hot, wet climates, and I run back to them. . . . Always seducing a lady or two . . . but really ravaging her first by pointing out to her the—what?—horrors?—Yes,horrors!—of the tropical country being conducted a tour through." On his "tours of God's world conducted by a minister of God," he had told Hannah in act 2, he is "collecting evidence" of his "personal idea of God." His story of human misery surviving on refuse in God's world is countered in act 3 by Hannah's travel story of human "acts of grace," in the House for the Dying in Shanghai, in which relatives of the dying poor ease their last moments through small tokens of kindness.

The contrast between the Eden-like Costa Verde and the hellish aspects of Shannon's tropics Hannah sees in human nature as well. "This veranda over the rain forest and the still-water beach, after long, difficult travels," she views as a stop along the way for those who must "keep on going." "And I don't mean just travels about the world, the earth's surface," she continues. "I mean . . . subterranean travels, the . . . the journeys that the spooked and bedeviled people are forced to take through the . . . *unlighted* sides of their natures" (all Williams's ellipses). When Shannon comments sardonically, "Don't tell me you have a dark side to your nature," Hannah replies, "I'm sure I don't have to tell a man as experienced and knowledgeable as you, Mr. Shannon, that everything has its shadowy side?"

A holiday party of Germans, a tank manufacturer and his family, are a reminder of the spreading shadowy side of world events in 1940. When Shannon first encounters them in act 1 he describes them as "a little animated cartoon by Hieronymus Bosch." Eating, drinking, joking, they tune in their short-wave radio continually to cheer the Nazi victories, and once the voice of Hitler (amid much static) intrudes upon the peaceful setting. Their childish glee provides an almost macabre comic relief, for they celebrate and sustain havoc and destruction. As they sing a marching song, their skin "an almost phosphorescent pink and gold color," Shannon observes, "Fiends out of hell with the . . . voices of . . . angels," to which Hannah adds, "Yes, they call it 'the logic of contradictions '" (both Williams's ellipses).

If the Costa Verde is Eden-like, the voluptuous Maxine is Eve, and the fruit she tempts Shannon with is a coconut shell filled with rum. Down-to-earth and uncomplicated compared to Shannon and Hannah, she is frank in her approach to him in their opening scene, asking, "Why don't you lay off the young ones and cultivate an interest in normal grown-up women?" In a letter to Bette Davis about her role of Maxine, Williams reveals his close attention to the details of production, including the actors' costumes and wigs:

> Everything about her should have the openness and freedom of the sea. . . . Death, life, it's all one to Maxine, she's a living definition of nature: lusty, rapacious, guileless, unsentimental. I think this creation of Maxine will be enormously helped when all the "externals" have been set right. . . . When she says "I never dress in September," I think she means just that. Her clothes shouldn't look as though they had just come from the laundry. . . . She moves with the ease of clouds and tides, her attitudes are free and relaxed.[7]

As the action draws to a close, Maxine invites Shannon to stay—"because I'm alone here now," she says.

Maxine is sympathetically portrayed as a lonely woman, despite her sexual indulgences with the two Mexican diving boys she hired when their former employer fired them "for being over-attentive to female guests." It is difficult to accept, except in the most literal sense, Louise Blackwell's classification of her, along with Serafina in *The Rose Tattoo,* as one of Williams's "women who have known happiness, but who have lost their mates and who try to overcome the loss." [8]

Maxine is tough because in her job she has to be, sizing up Hannah and Nonno as penniless, sensing the "vibrations" between Shannon and Hannah, and putting her in a room with a leaking roof. But the quiet Hannah is more than a match for her, accepting the room, maintaining her dignity, and even threatening in act 2 to walk to the town "ten miles, with a storm coming up," pushing her grandfather in his wheelchair, when Maxine accuses her of being "a deadbeat, using that dying old man for a front to get in places without the cash to pay even one day in advance."

Both Shannon and Hannah bluff to survive; so does Maxine. As act 2 opens, she tells Hannah that when her husband, Fred, died, "He'd left me in such a financial hole that if living didn't mean more to me than money, I'd might as well have been dropped in the ocean with him." Hannah has none of Maxine's jealousy and even points out to Shannon in their long night's talk that he could do worse than remaining at the hotel.

While Maxine is the tempter and Hannah the preserver of Shannon, Miss Fellowes tries very hard to be the destroyer. She is one of Williams's rare unredeemed characters, like Jabe in *Orpheus Descending*. But she is not a motiveless hating character: her cruelty, rather, is prompted by sexual jealousy, her lesbian attachment to Charlotte, who has declared her love for Shannon.

THE NIGHT OF THE IGUANA

Two positive developments lift the play's ending and sound a note of hope. One is the completion of Nonno's poem, of which snatches have been heard throughout and which he finally recites in its entirety. It is a good poem. Its theme of death, desire, and rebirth is "minor poet" Williams at his best. The orange on the branch dies calmly, knowing its fall to earth will be followed by decay but also by rebirth from this "intercourse not well designed / For beings of a golden kind." While resurrection is a recurring theme in Williams's plays, this is the first in which death is accepted and faced with dignity, not fled from as a feared pursuer.

Another positive feature is that the iguana, a symbol of Shannon, gains its freedom in act 3. As described by Williams in the short story of the same name, from which the play evolved, "The Iguana is a lizard, two or three feet in length. . . . What bothered her . . . was the inhumanity of its treatment. . . . hitched to the base of the column . . . and making the most pitiful effort to scramble into the bushes just beyond the taut length of its rope."[9]

Shannon recognizes the plight of the iguana as analogous when he reveals it with his flashlight: "See? The iguana? At the end of its rope? Trying to go on past the end of its goddam rope? Like *you!* Like *me!* Like Grampa with his last poem!" Shannon also is trussed up like the iguana, held in the hammock by ropes from which he will physically free himself, just as Hannah's quiet truths free him emotionally from his panic. In cutting the iguana loose in act 3, at Hannah's insistence that it is "able to feel pain and panic" as one of God's creatures, Shannon says he is doing so "because God won't do it and we are going to play God here." He calls freeing the iguana "a little act of grace."

Simultaneously, Nonno completes and recites his poem. Shannon and Maxine go off on a night swim, and Hannah, not realizing Nonno is dead, is left alone onstage in the play's final moments. She asks: "Oh, God, can't we stop now? Finally? Please let us. It's so quiet here, now." Shannon had asked earlier what she would do "when the old gentleman goes." Hannah's reply was: "Stop or go on . . . probably go on" (Williams's ellipsis).

The ending is somewhat ambiguous. Joining Maxine for a swim and leaving Hannah, Shannon seems to indicate his immediate future: "I stay here, I reckon, and live off la patrona." When he had asked Hannah to travel with him she had called his suggestion impractical. But in act 2, when she is sketching Shannon, Hannah says, "I have a strong feeling you will go back to the Church." She hopes that when he does he will show some human compassion for his parishioners, who are seeking "something to still believe in," and that he will "lead them beside still waters because you know how badly they need the still waters, Mr. Shannon." Throughout the play he has been trying to write to his bishop, to apologize and ask for a post. While Maxine derides these efforts, Hannah believes in them, for, even though in act 3 she accepts his gold cross to hock for her passage back to the States, she says she will mail him the pawn ticket so he can redeem it (as she has tried to redeem him). "You'll want it again, when you've gotten over your fever," she tells him.

In act 3, when Shannon is tied up in the hammock, giving what Hannah describes as a "Passion Play performance," she observes, "Who wouldn't like to suffer and atone for the sins of himself and the world if it could be done in a hammock with ropes instead of nails, on a hill that's so much lovelier than Golgotha?" This has led some commentators to see Shannon as a symbol of Christ. Yet Hannah's comment is ironic; actually, she is the more likely symbol, as Rogers points out: "If there is any Christ figure in *The Night of the Iguana,* it is Hannah. With her patience, gentleness, endurance and compassion, she carries the true Christian message." Rogers observes further that "Williams's morality is strikingly Christian": "He demands loving commitment to all men." [10]

A symphony of sounds evokes the lyric atmosphere of the exotic Costa Verde. Although a marimba band may be heard occasionally, carried by the wind from the beach, the varied score is drawn from nature rather than from formal music: bird calls, wind, rain, the sea, and the crescendo of the storm. As it approaches, toward the end of act 2, Williams describes the musical effect he seeks: "This part of the scene, which is played in a 'scherzo' mood, has an accompanying windy obbligato on the hilltop—all through it we hear the wind . . . gradually rising . . . and there are fitful glimmers of lightning in the sky."

Contributing to the symphony of sound are the rhythm, idiom, and cadence of the dialogue, which also reveals individual character. Maxine "always laughs with a single harsh, loud bark." The rhythmic quality of Shannon's speeches reminds us that he has been a preacher: "I've just been hanging on till I could get in this hammock on this veranda over the rain forest and the still-water beach," he tells Maxine as she is shaving him in act 1. But the strident staccato of Miss Fellowes's accusations breaks Shannon's rhythm, reducing him to a spondaic outcry: "Don't! Break! *Human! Pride!*" The Germans contribute to the score their guttural cries of delight, and their sputtering radio carries Hitler's speech to the Reichstag: "A human voice like a mad dog's bark emerges from the static momentarily."

Williams describes this play as "a dramatic poem of the most intensely personal nature." [11] Even the stage directions are poetic: the arrival of the iguana and the coming of the storm in act 2 are heralded by "a windy sound in the rain forest and a flicker of gold light like a silent scattering of gold coins on the veranda; then the sound of shouting voices." Williams displays his artistry with sound effects, as silence is followed by shouts. The Mexican boys, who have captured the iguana, raise a "commotion" in Spanish, and Maxine joins in. Tied up, the iguana creates a "scrap-

ing, scuffling sound." Even the ugly iguana, Hannah points
out, is "one of God's creatures," just as the grandeur of
nature also is symbolic of God. Williams's recurrent symbol of water as purification is suggested by the rain and the
still-water beach. The latter also is reminiscent of the
Twenty-third Psalm, with its quiet melodies echoed in
Hannah's speeches.

Hannah's dialogue reflects her character: calm, cool,
proper. Her idiom is formal, as if designed to discourage
intimacy. As Williams notes during the long conversation
in act 3, "Hannah has always had a sort of fastidiousness,
a reluctance, toward intimate physical contact." She addresses Shannon as "Mr.Shannon," and he instinctively
calls her "Miss Jelkes," although he is on a first-name basis
with everyone except Miss Fellowes. (Williams's proper
names, like hers and Maxine's, are often descriptive puns.)
To Shannon's observation at the end of act 2—"I'm going
to tell you something about yourself. You are a lady, a *real*
one and a *great* one"—Hannah replies with characteristic
formality, "What have I done to merit that compliment
from you?"

For characters who are "different," like Hannah,
Blanche, and Alma, Williams will heighten natural speech
to achieve a lyric effect through diction, rhythm, and
repetition, although each of these ladies has her unique
idiom. In her third-act aria Hannah tells Shannon:

I was young once, Mr. Shannon, but I was one of those people who can be young without really having their youth, and not to have your youth when you are young is naturally very disturbing. But I was lucky. My work, this occupational therapy that I gave myself— painting and doing quick character sketches—made me look out of myself, not in, and gradually, at the far end of the tunnel that I was struggling out of I began to see this faint, very faint gray light—the light of the world outside me—and I kept climbing toward it. I had to.

In this speech the words are everyday ones, unlike the literary, almost quaint diction that sets Blanche and Alma apart. The substance of Hannah's speeches matches the style, expressed rhythmically and emphasizing key words with repetition, while reflecting onomatopoeically a character moving toward a goal. The short sentences, after long ones that hesitate, interrupt, and weigh choices, convey Hannah's clear-eyed determination to accept, not evade, reality, as Shannon has done.

"Hannah" and "Shannon" sound alike, and perhaps each is incomplete, a half-person lacking an essential quality possessed by the other. Hannah shrinks from physical contact, but intellectually and emotionally she is instantly and instinctively able to communicate with others. Shannon, on the other hand, can relate to women only on the physical level. Emotionally, his sense of sin for his sexual encounters torments him and drives him to seek escape in drink. The "vibrations" between the two which Maxine senses Hannah terms "our . . . sympathetic interest in each other," which Maxine "seems to have misunderstood" (Williams's ellipsis).

Perhaps their long talk on the veranda in act 3 can teach Shannon the lesson Hannah has had to learn—to look out of oneself, "not in." Above all, she values human communication and understanding. She tells Shannon she believes in "broken gates between people so they can reach each other, even if it's just for one night only. . . . A little understanding exchanged between them, a wanting to help each other through nights like this." Williams says in *Memoirs* that loneliness has been his constant theme. In this play he demonstrates that isolation, symbolized by the "cells," or cubicles, of the hotel, can be overcome by reaching out to another with understanding. Earlier he had stated that "life achieves its highest value and significance . . . when two lives are confluent, when the walls of isolation momentarily collapse between two persons." [12]

Appreciating that Hannah "can't stand to be touched," Shannon asks during their long conversation if they might "*travel* together, I mean just *travel* together?" But Hannah is realistic, even though this could be a solution for both of them: "I think the impracticality of the idea will appear much clearer to you in the morning, Mr. Shannon." Because of her generous nature, she even points out the consolation of what he regards as "winding up with the . . . inconsolable widow," as she reminds him that "we all wind up with something or with someone, and if it's someone instead of just something, we're lucky, perhaps . . . unusually lucky" (both Williams's ellipses).

This last major work does not end in violence or destruction. The death of Jonathan Coffin (Nonno) is peaceful, and the poem he completes carries the hope of rebirth. The iguana is freed, as Shannon is from his spook, though release may be temporary for both. Hannah will "probably go on."

Despite its uneven production, *The Night of the Iguana* was acclaimed when it opened on Broadway at the end of 1961 and at the beginning of Williams's "lost decade." Although in Chicago Claudia Cassidy had claimed that "Tennessee Williams has written a bankrupt play," the New York critics were enthusiastic. Henry Hewes wrote: "There it is. Destruction and creation, cruelty and compassion, smut and spirituality, all of the paradoxical ingredients so essential to the divine equation Mr. Williams uses to transform energy into living stage matter. And again he does so with the same style, humor, and sensitivity that make him the foremost American playwright of his time." [13] The play was judged best of the season by the Drama Critics' Circle and was purchased by MGM for a film version. As the ultimate accolade, Williams, whose plays frequently had been derided and described as a "fetid swamp" in *Time,* now appeared on the cover of that magazine, which proclaimed him "the greatest U.S. playwright since Eugene O'Neill, and barring the aged Sean O'Casey, the greatest living playwright anywhere." [14]

Bette Davis, who was cast as Maxine, had immediately taken exception to director Frank Corsaro, more reputed for broad comedy than for subtle drama, and she had insisted that he be dismissed during the Chicago tryout. According to the agreement, however, he would retain program credit for the direction; thus, there was no overall style or continuity, no artistic entity to which each actor could contribute. Williams, who accompanied the production on the road, as was his usual practice, worked at rewriting the script in the mornings for afternoon rehearsals.

The cast presented a series of one-dimensional vignettes—Miss Davis mostly strident as Maxine but lacking depth and sensuality and Patrick O'Neal as Shannon more puzzled than despairing. Only Alan Webb as Nonno and Margaret Leighton in a sensitive, poetic interpretation of Hannah were able to realize Williams's depths of characterization. Walter Kerr praised Hannah's "placid, overriding authority . . . the knot of her will . . . the suppressed warmth, the leashed radiance, that glows within a composed facade but is forbidden to display itself or to spend itself." Kerr recognized that Williams's "artistry was aided in production . . . by a performance from Margaret Leighton which was so intangibly spun and so mysteriously self-contained as to cause one to dismiss as mechanical exhibitionism most of the work that is done weekly on our stages." [15]

Directed by John Huston, the 1964 film is really two works—a commonplace, non-Williams prologue in which all of the exposition is acted out, followed by an abridged version of the play. Shannon's provocative sermon and subsequent dismissal are followed by a long sequence in which he swims with Charlotte and seduces her in his room. The cast is excellent. Richard Burton conveys the character of a disintegrating Shannon clinging to the last vestiges of dignity. Ava Gardner endows Maxine with the sexuality so important to the character and to the play's suggestion that she and Hannah are opposite extremes, profane and sacred love. Deborah Kerr is an appealing Hannah. The film preserves a faithful if condensed version of the play, especially if one begins to view it one-third of the way along, with the arrival of the bus at the Costa Verde. Characteristic of Hollywood, the ending is not ambiguous.

Exemplifying the success of the British in interpreting Williams was the 1992 presentation of *The Night of the Iguana* by the Royal National Theatre. Directed by Richard Eyre, it was not only the dramatic high point of that London season but also the first major production of this play to fully realize its complex values. Here was the plastic theater Williams longed for, with Bob Crowley's setting of the faded red wood veranda dominated and overwhelmed by huge tropical foliage reminiscent of Rousseau. A ramp the width of the orchestra pit became the hill up which visitors arrived. The scrim walls of the three cubicles, backlit from time to time, revealed an inner dimension, achieving, as Williams directed, the effect of a "little interior stage, the curtains giving a misty effect to their dim inside lighting."

Fine ensemble playing orchestrated the text, with the "cartoon" German family a comic scherzo, the storm at the end of act 2 a fierce crescendo of thunder and lightning illuminating Shannon's reaching-out hands, and the melodies of Hannah's third-act arias a quiet coda before an audience spellbound by Williams's magic. Through his size and his skill Alfred Molina brought epic proportions to a tormented Shannon, moving from nervous exhaustion to rage to acceptance. He was perfectly balanced by Eileen Atkins's many-faceted Hannah. With a minimum of voice, stance, and gesture (in contrast to Molina's controlled extravagance), she revealed vulnerability beneath a seemingly imperturbable exterior.

The Night of the Iguana is the last of Williams's major plays. Never again would a work attain the artistic and commercial success so important to Williams. But, like Hannah Jelkes, he continued to "go on," writing every day, struggling with his spooks. In the final account he left at least nine great stage works and played a major role in revolutionizing the American theater by breaking the stranglehold of realism: the Broadway stage became boundless, and theatergoers could appreciate not only Tennessee Williams but also David Mamet, Edward Albee, Harold Pinter, and Samuel Beckett.

Notes

1. Tennessee Williams, *Memoirs* (Garden City, N.Y.: Doubleday, 1975), 182–83.

2. Tennessee Williams, "A Summer of Discovery," *Where I Live: Selected Essays,* ed. Christine R. Day and Bob Woods (New York: New Directions, 1978), 147.

3. Cecil Brown, "Interview with Tennessee Williams," *Conversations with Tennessee Williams,* ed. Albert J. Devlin (Jackson: University Press of Mississippi, 1986), 266.

4. Esther Merle Jackson, "Tennessee Williams," in *The American Theatre Today,* ed. Alan S. Downer (New York: Basic Books, 1967), 83.

5. Ingrid Rogers, *Tennessee Williams: A Moralist's Answer to the Perils of Life* (Frankfurt: Peter Lang, 1976), 130.

6. Williams, "Summer of Discovery," 137–47.

7. Quoted in *Five O'Clock Angel: Letters of Tennessee Williams to Maria St. Just, 1948–1982,* ed. Maria St. Just (New York: Alfred A. Knopf, 1990), 176.

8. Louise Blackwell, "Tennessee Williams and the Predicament of Women," *South Atlantic Bulletin* 35 (March 1970): 14.

THE NIGHT OF THE IGUANA

9. *Tennessee Williams: Collected Stories* (New York: New Directions, 1985; London: Secker and Warburg, 1985), 234–35.

10. Rogers, *Tennessee Williams,* 110–11.

11. Cheryl Crawford, "Four by Tenn," *One Naked Individual: My Fifty Years in the Theatre* (New York: Bobbs-Merrill, 1977), 199.

12. Tennessee Williams, "The Human Psyche—Alone, *Where I Live,* 36–37.

13. Henry Hewes, "El Purgatorio," *Saturday Review of Literature* 45, 20 January 1962, 36.

14. "The Angel of the Odd," *Time* 79, 9 March 1962, 53–56, 59, 60.

15. Walter Kerr, "Mr. Williams," *The Theatre in Spite of Itself* (New York: Simon and Schuster, 1963), 253.

BIBLIOGRAPHY

Primary Works

Plays

The standard edition of the plays is *The Theatre of Tennessee Williams,* published in eight volumes by New Directions, 1971–1992.

Camino Real. New York: New Directions, 1953.

Cat on a Hot Tin Roof. New York: New Directions, 1955. London: Penguin Books, 1957.

The Glass Menagerie. New York: New Directions, 1945. New York: Dramatists Play Service, 1948 (acting edition).

I Rise in Flame Cried the Phoenix. New York: Dramatists Play Service, 1951. In *The Theatre of Tennessee Williams.* Vol. 7. New York: New Directions, 1981.

The Night of the Iguana. New York: New Directions, 1962. London: Penguin Books, 1964.

Orpheus Descending, with Battle of Angels. New York: New Directions, 1958.

Orpheus Descending. In *Tennessee Williams: Five Plays.* London: Secker and Warburg, 1958.

The Rose Tattoo. New York: New Directions, 1951.

A Streetcar Named Desire. New York: New Directions, 1947. In *Tennessee Williams: Four Plays.* London: Secker and Warburg, 1956. New York: Dramatists Play Service, 1953 (acting edition).

BIBLIOGRAPHY

Summer and Smoke and the Eccentricities of a Nightingale.
New York: New Directions, 1964.
Summer and Smoke. In *Tennessee Williams: Four Plays.*
London: Secker and Warburg, 1956.
Sweet Bird of Youth. New York: New Directions, 1959. In
Tennessee Williams: Four Plays. London: Secker and
Warburg, 1956.

Fiction

Tennessee Williams: Collected Stories. New York: New
Directions, 1985. London: Secker and Warburg, 1985.

Poetry

Five Young American Poets. Norfolk, Conn.: New Directions, 1944.
In the Winter of Cities. Norfolk, Conn.: New Directions,
1956.

Autobiography

Memoirs. Garden City, N.Y.: Doubleday, 1975.

Essays

Where I Live: Selected Essays. Edited by Christine R. Day
and Bob Woods. New York: New Directions, 1978.

Letters

Five O'Clock Angel: Letters of Tennessee Williams to Maria St. Just, 1948–1982. With commentary by Maria St. Just. New York: Alfred A. Knopf, 1990. Invaluable record of Williams's views written to a trusted friend during his creative years.

Letters to Donald Windham, 1940–1965. Edited by Donald Windham. New York: Holt, Rinehart and Winston, 1976.

Interviews

Conversations with Tennessee Williams. Edited by Albert J. Devlin. Jackson: University Press of Mississippi, 1986. A good selection of interviews, including some that Williams later disclaimed.

Secondary Works

Biography

Dictionary of Literary Biography Documentary Series: Tennessee Williams. Edited by Margaret A. Van Antwerp and Sally Johns. Detroit: Gale Research, 1984.

Leavitt, Richard F., ed. *The World of Tennessee Williams.* New York: Putnam's, 1978.

BIBLIOGRAPHY

Williams, Edwina Dakin (as told to Lucy Freeman). *Remember Me to Tom.* New York: Putnam's, 1963.

Bibliography

Gunn, Drewey Wayne. *Tennessee Williams: A Bibliography.* Metuchen, N.J.: Scarecrow Press, 1980. Useful compilation includes reviews and unpublished manuscripts.

McCann, John S. *The Critical Reputation of Tennessee Williams: A Reference Guide.* Boston: G. K. Hall, 1983. Annotated, with helpful descriptions of books and articles.

Critical Studies: Books

Adler, Thomas P. *A Streetcar Named Desire: The Moth and the Lantern.* Boston: G. K. Hall, 1990. Perceptive analysis.

Bigsby, C. W. E. *A Critical Introduction to Twentieth-Century American Drama.* Vol. 2: *Tennessee Williams / Arthur Miller / Edward Albee.* Cambridge: Cambridge University Press, 1984. Important evaluation of the works, including unpublished material.

Bloom, Harold., ed. *The Glass Menagerie: Modern Critical Interpretations.* New York: Chelsea House, 1988.

———, ed. *A Streetcar Named Desire: Modern Critical Interpretations.* New York: Chelsea House, 1988.

———, ed. *Tennessee Williams: Modern Critical Views.* New York: Chelsea House, 1987.

Boxill, Roger. *Tennessee Williams*. London: Macmillan, 1986. Conjectures pasts of characters classified as "wanderers," or "faded belles," Williams as oedipal victim.

Falk, Signi L. *Tennessee Williams*. New York: Twayne Publishers, 1961. Prudish, superficial early study. Revised but not improved in 1978.

Fedder, Norman J. *The Influence of D. H. Lawrence on Tennessee Williams*. The Hague: Mouton, 1966. Williams's application of Laurentian theories about sex.

File on Tennessee Williams (handbook). Compiled by Catherine M. Arnott. London: Methuen, 1985. Chronology, facts on each published play, review excerpts.

Heilman, Robert B. *The Iceman, the Arsonist, and the Troubled Agent: Tragedy and Melodrama on the Modern Stage*. Seattle: University of Washington Press, 1973. A master applies his dramatic theories to Williams.

Huizinga, Johan. *Homo Ludens: A Study of the Play-Element in Culture*. London: Routledge and Kegan Paul, 1949. Important classic study.

Jackson, Esther Merle. *The Broken World of Tennessee Williams*. Madison: University of Wisconsin Press, 1965. Study of the sociological, psychological, religious, and philosophical influences on Williams's imagery.

Kazan, Elia. *A Life*. New York: Alfred A. Knopf, 1988. The director of four of the major plays writes of his theater associations with Williams.

BIBLIOGRAPHY

Ley-Piscator, Maria. *The Piscator Experiment.* New York: James H. Heineman, 1967.

Londre, Felicia. *Tennessee Williams.* New York: Frederick Ungar, 1979. Plot synopses and critical quotes from papers, including the tabloids.

Murphy, Brenda. *Tennessee Williams and Elia Kazan: A Collaboration in the Theatre.* Cambridge: Cambridge University Press, 1992. Gives Kazan even more credit than he claims for Williams's artistic success. Unconvincing.

Nelson, Benjamin. *Tennessee Williams: The Man and His Work.* New York: Ivan Obolensky, 1961. Interesting early study.

Pauly, Thomas H. *An American Odyssey: Elia Kazan and American Culture.* Philadelphia: Temple University Press, 1983.

Presley, Delma E. *The Glass Menagerie: An American Memory.* Boston: G. K. Hall, 1990. Perceptive in-depth study.

Rogers, Ingrid. *Tennessee Williams: A Moralist's Answer to the Perils of Life.* Frankfurt: Peter Lang, 1976. Important first full-length study of Williams as a moral playwright.

Shaland, Irene. *Tennessee Williams on the Soviet Stage.* Lanham, Md.: University Press of America, 1987. Useful revelation of varied interpretations of Williams's work.

Stanton, Stephen S., ed. *Tennessee Williams: A Collection of Critical Essays.* Englewood Cliffs, N.J.: Prentice-Hall, 1977. A collection of "thesis" approaches.

Tharpe, Jac, ed. *Tennessee Williams: A Tribute.* Jackson: University Press of Mississippi, 1977. The best collection of scholars' original essays, fifty-two in all.

Thompson, Judith J. *Tennessee Williams's Plays: Memory, Myth, and Symbol.* New York: Peter Lang, 1987. Classical and archetypical allusions in Williams's symbolism.

Tischler, Nancy M. *Tennessee Williams: Rebellious Puritan.* New York: Citadel Press, 1963. Explores Williams's self-confessed mixture of Puritanism and romanticism.

Weales, Gerald. *Tennessee Williams.* Minneapolis: University of Minnesota Press, 1965. Short, excellent overview.

Yacowar, Maurice. *Tennessee Williams and Film.* New York: Frederick Ungar, 1977.

Zeineddine, Nada. *Because It Is My Name.* Braunton and Devon, U.K.: Merlin Books, 1991. Impressive exploration of the identity crisis in Williams's women.

Critical Studies: Articles and Chapters in Books

Bennett, Beate Hein. "Williams and European Drama: Infernalists and Forgers of Modern Myths." In *Tennessee Willliams: A Tribute,* edited by Jac Tharpe, 429–59. Jackson: University Press of Mississippi, 1977.

BIBLIOGRAPHY

Bentley, Eric. "A Streetcar Named Desire." *In Search of Theatre.* New York: Vintage Books, 1959.

Blackwell, Louise. "Tennessee Williams and the Predicament of Women." *South Atlantic Bulletin* 35 (March 1970): 9–14.

Borny, Geoffrey. "The Two *Glass Menageries:* Reading Edition and Acting Edition." In *The Glass Menagerie: Modern Critical Interpretations,* edited by Harold Bloom, 101–17. New York: Chelsea House, 1988.

Brandt, George. "Cinematic Structure in the Work of Tennessee Williams." *American Theatre,* Stratford-on-Avon Studies, 10:163–88. London: Edward Arnold, 1967.

Brown, Cecil. "Interview with Tennessee Williams." *Partisan Review* 45 (1978). Reprinted in *Conversations with Tennessee Williams,* edited by Albert J. Devlin, 251–83. Jackson: University Press of Mississippi, 1986.

Browne, E. Martin. "Editorial Note." *Cat on a Hot Tin Roof.* London: Penguin Books, 1957.

Brustein, Robert. "America's New Culture Hero: Feelings without Words." In *A Streetcar Named Desire: Modern Critical Interpretations,* edited by Harold Bloom, 7–16. New York: Chelsea House, 1988.

Clurman, Harold. "Tennessee Williams." *The Divine Pastime: Theatre Essays.* New York: Macmillan, 1974. Solid reviews of first Williams productions.

Cohn, Ruby. "The Garrulous Grotesques of Tennessee Williams." *Dialogue in American Drama.* Bloomington: Indiana University Press, 1971. Williams's poetry falls on deaf ears.

Crawford, Cheryl. "Four by Tenn." *One Naked Individual: My Fifty Years in the Theatre.* New York: Bobbs-Merrill, 1977.

Freedley, George (interview). "The Role of Poetry in the Modern Theatre." In *Conversations with Tennessee Williams,* edited by Albert J. Devlin, 20–24. Jackson: University Press of Mississippi, 1986.

Ganz, Arthur. "A Desperate Morality." In *Tennessee Williams: Modern Critical Views,* edited by Harold Bloom, 99–111. New York: Chelsea House, 1987.

Gelb, Arthur. "Williams and Kazan and the Big Walk-Out." *New York Times,* 1 May 1960.

Hafley, James. "Abstraction and Order in the Language of Tennessee Williams." In *Tennessee Williams: A Tribute,* edited by Jac Tharpe, 753–62. Jackson: University Press of Mississippi, 1977.

Jackson, Esther Merle. "Tennessee Williams." In *The American Theatre Today,* edited by Alan S. Downer, 73–84. New York: Basic Books, 1967.

Kazan, Elia. "Notebook for 'A Streetcar Named Desire.'" In *Directors on Directing: A Source Book of the Modern Theatre,* edited by Toby Cole and Helen Krich Chinoy, 364–79. Indianapolis: Bobbs-Merrill, 1963.

BIBLIOGRAPHY

Kerr, Walter. "Mr. Williams." *The Theatre in Spite of Itself.* New York: Simon and Schuster, 1963. Outstanding analysis of *Night of the Iguana* by a critic and director.

McCarthy, Mary. "A Streetcar Called Success." *Sights and Spectacles, 1937–1956.* New York: Farrar, Straus, Cudahy, 1956.

Mamet, David. "Realism." *Writing in Restaurants.* New York: Viking Penguin, 1986. Demolishes "method" acting of the 1950s.

———— "Tennessee Williams: March 26th, 1911–February 25th, 1983." *Rolling Stone,* 14 April 1983, 124.

Miller, Arthur. "The Shadows of the Gods." *The Theater Essays of Arthur Miller.* Edited by Robert A. Martin. New York: Viking Press, 1978. Williams's great contemporary interprets *Cat on a Hot Tin Roof.*

————. "Tennessee Williams's Legacy," *TV Guide,* 3 March 1984.

Nathan, George Jean. "The Rose Tattoo." *The Theatre Book of the Year, 1950–51.* New York: Alfred A. Knopf, 1951. More acerbic than perceptive.

Pease, Donald. "Reflections on Moon Lake: The Presences of the Playwright." In *Tennessee Williams: A Tribute,* edited by Jac Tharpe, 829–47. Jackson: University Press of Mississippi, 1977.

Popkin, Henry. "The Plays of Tennessee Williams," *Tulane Drama Review* 4 (Spring 1960): 45–64.

Porter, Thomas E. "The Passing of the Old South." *Myth*

and Modern American Drama. Detroit: Wayne State
University Press, 1969.

Rader, Dotson (interview). "The Art of Theatre V: Tennessee Williams." *Paris Review* (Fall 1981). Reprinted in
Conversations with Tennessee Williams, edited by Albert
J. Devlin, 325–60. Jackson: University Press of Mississippi, 1986.

Sievers, W. David. "Tennessee Williams and Arthur Miller."
*Freud on Broadway: A History of Psychoanalysis and
the American Drama.* New York: Cooper Square Publishers, 1955. Classic and convincing.

Styan, John L. "On Tears and Laughter: *The Rose Tattoo.*"
2d ed. *The Dark Comedy: The Development of Modern
Comic Tragedy.* Cambridge: Cambridge University
Press, 1968.

Tischler, Nancy M. "The Distorted Mirror: Tennessee
Williams's Self-Portraits." *Mississippi Quarterly* 25
(Fall 1972): 389–403.

Waters, Arthur. "Tennessee Williams Ten Years Later."
Theatre Arts (July 1955): 72–73, 96.

INDEX

INDEX

INDEX

INDEX

INDEX

The Library of Congress has cataloged the cloth edition as follows:
Griffin, Alice, 1924–
    Understanding Tennessee Williams / by Alice Griffin.
        p. cm.—(Understanding contemporary American literature)
    Includes bibliographical references and index.
    Contents: Understanding Tennessee Williams—The glass menagerie—A
streetcar named Desire—Summer and smoke—The rose tattoo—Camino
Real—Cat on a hot tin roof—Orpheus descending—Sweet bird of youth—
The night of the iguana.
    ISBN 1-57003-017-0
    1. Williams, Tennessee, 1911–1983—Criticism and interpretation.
I. Title. II. Series.
PS3545.I5365 Z664   1995
812'.54—dc20   94—18690
                                      CIP

CPSIA information can be obtained
at www.ICGtesting.com
Printed in the USA
FFOW04n1453270315
12194FF

9 781611 170061